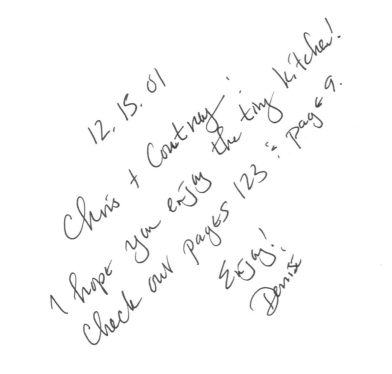

12.15.01

Chris + Courtney :

1 hope you enjoy the tiny kitchen!
Check our pages 123 ". Page 9.

Enjoy!
Denise

the tiny kitchen

the tiny kitchen
cooking and entertaining

by denise sullivan medved

photography by jeri pinson wellens

illustrations by todd healy

TINY KITCHEN PUBLISHING   2001

Published by Tiny Kitchen Publishing.

For information write Tiny Kitchen Publishing, 5115 Ravensworth Road, Annandale, VA 22003

thetinykitchen@aol.com

www.thetinykitchen.com

FIRST EDITION
Designed by Denise Sullivan Medved
Photography by Jeri Pinson Wellens
Illustrations by Todd Healy

ISBN 0-9716028-0-8

Dedicated to my husband BILL,
who has encouraged me through the wide variety of
projects I start, most of which I have never finished!

contents

acknowledgments

i would like to express my gratitude and appreciation for all those who contributed to *the tiny kitchen*:

My husband Bill. I can't begin to thank him for his love and support, especially the day I called him and told him I couldn't stand my job one more day and I had to quit. He encouraged me to do it right then and there. This book wouldn't have come to fruition had I not quit my job. For all of his contributions in the capacity of editor, sharing his recipes, advice on design and layout, and acting as cook and crew for the photo shoot.

My family. My parents, Bob and Kay Sullivan; sister, Missy; brother-in-law, Bob; niece, Katie and, nephew, Matthew for their encouragement, support and enthusiasm.

Grandmas Dexter and Sullivan for getting me started in my own kitchen by handing down recipes and equipment.

Jeri Pinson Wellens, my cousin, who graciously offered her photography services; the resulting pictures far exceeding my expectations.

Todd Healy, my friend, for designing the cover illustration and for lending me his Captain's Row illustration for the back cover.

Paul Mattioli, for encouraging me to buy the book *Getting Your Book Published for Dummies* and also for encouraging me to leave the company we worked at.

Richard Rossi, my friend, who lent me Dan Sullivan's motivational tapes.

Lowell (The Senator) and Claudia Weicker for their enthusiasm and support.

Oprah's Lifestyle Makeover Program. Without hearing the stories of others who tossed away high paying jobs to do something they loved, *I* wouldn't have.

Fairfax County Public Library. Their resources were instrumental in my research for how to write a cookbook and in understanding the publishing industry.

All of my friends and relatives who have made my parties over the years so much fun for me. Without great guests, you can't have a great party!

Alex	Craig	Jennifer	Lizz	Sarah
Alice	Darryl	Jenny	Loretta	Scott
Amy	Dawn	Jeri	Lorraine	Sherri
AnaMarie	Deb	Jerry	Lowell	Skip
Anh	Debbie	Jill	Madge	Stacy
Anne	Deirdre	Jillian	Mark	Stephen
Art	Delia	Jimmy	Mary	Stevie
Ashley	Dolan	JoAnn	Mary Jane	Susan
Beth	Edward	John	Matthew	Susie
Bill	Ellie	Kara	Michael	Ted
Bob	Emilia	Karen	Michelle	Terry
Bobby	Ernie	Kathleen	Mike	Therese
Bridgette	Gene	Kathy	Missy	Tizzy
Bruce	George	Kathy Ann	Moira	Watty
Bubba	Ginny	Katie	Nancy	
Caroline	Giuliana	Kay	Pat	And to
Carter	Greg	Keith	Patty	everyone
Cheryl	Gretchen	Kenneth	Paul	I may
Chris	Ian	Larry	Peter	have
Chuck	Jack	Leah	Richard	forgotten,
Cindy	Jake	Linda	Robin	I apologize.
Claudia	Jeff	Lisa	Santé	

And last, but certainly not least, St. Anthony, St. Rita and St. Jude for hearing and answering my prayers and novenas to make the idea of *the tiny kitchen* a reality. They have never let me down!

introduction

just imagine throwing a cocktail party for seventy-five or a sit down dinner for twenty in a small one bedroom Manhattan apartment and preparing all the food yourself in a kitchen not much bigger than a broom closet—*a tiny kitchen*. Well, these are just two of the dozens of parties my roommates and I had while living in Apartment 2C in the Leonore at 63rd and Madison back in the 1980's. And, I did it all with very limited kitchen equipment—just a couple of pots and pans, a few bowls, a grater, manual eggbeater and other basic utensils which were handed down to me from my Grandma Dexter.

Cooking and entertaining have always been a part of my life. And probably, like most, I began by helping my mother in the kitchen. I was eight, and have been cooking ever since. I love the satisfaction of creating a dish from scratch, setting the dinner table and enjoying the meal. It is especially rewarding to see the smiles on my friends' and families' faces after a good meal or during a party.

I guess since I started cooking and entertaining so early it's second nature to me. I've always considered it easy and fun! While growing up, my parents routinely entertained small and large crowds with elegance and finesse. They taught me well.

As a twenty-something single, young professional, I moved to Manhattan with aspirations of making the big bucks, but the reality was that in the beginning I had limited means. Like many in my situation, I was forced to live in a small apartment with roommates. The first year I moved three times before finally settling into Apartment 2C in The Leonore for four years. With each move my location improved, but the rent went up and the apartment got smaller. The Leonore was a great location, but it was small. Thus the challenge began, how do you cook and entertain in a tiny kitchen, gracefully?

Picture the kind of kitchen I am referring to—an oven too small to hold even a small turkey; a stove-top where if the burners were any closer together they would be on top of each other; a refrigerator that's about two-thirds of the size of your mom's, a single sink, a couple of cabinets and drawers, and one-foot of counter space. Forget about a dishwasher, icemaker, microwave and garbage disposal. And no room (or budget, for that matter) for any fancy equipment like a food processor, industrial mixer, the latest cookware, or cutlery (that's what wedding showers are for!).

Often I would be preparing for a party, dinner, or just something new to fix for my friends, so I'd flip through cookbooks for new ideas. (I read cookbooks like others read novels or the newspaper). Sure there were some great recipes, but many called for elaborate equipment like you see on the cooking shows. I would keep turning the pages until I found recipes I could either make in my tiny kitchen or could adapt to the supplies and space I had. It was limiting and frustrating and it was at this time I wondered why there were no cookbooks focusing on a tiny kitchen. Thus, the seed was planted.

There were many charity events on the social calendar such as The Kips Bay Boys and Girls Club, Martha Graham Dance Company, The Big Apple Circus and The Fresh Air Fund of which my friends and I were active members of the junior committees. We frequently had cocktail parties before the events at good ol' Apartment 2C. Despite the limited prep space and a small budget, people always seemed to have a great time and were amazed at the foods I whipped up with such limitations. This was always enhanced by the nice silver serving pieces I inherited from Grandma Dexter. Presentation is key.

In 1989 I packed my bags and moved back to my native Alexandria, Virginia. I found the perfect apartment on Prince Street in Old Town. Prince Street is an old cobblestone street one block off the Potomac River. This block is referred to as

Captain's Row. Its river proximity made it an ideal location for sea captains of the early 1700's to settle down. My apartment was the second story of a town house originally built in the 1700's. It had lots of charm with the original wide plank pine floors still in tact, however, at a slant due to settling over the years. The thirteen-foot ceilings and working fireplaces in each the living room, library and bedroom added to the character and charm. These rooms were huge. Somewhere along the line when it had been converted into its own apartment back in the 1930's, a bathroom and kitchen were added. The bathroom was a decent size; but the kitchen was converted from either a tiny closet or hidden doorway as it was squeezed in between the library and bedroom. I thought my kitchen at the Leonore in Manhattan was small, this space redefined the term "tiny kitchen." Two people literally could not stand in the kitchen at the same time. There was one cabinet, below the one-foot counter top, one drawer and a couple of makeshift shelves above the stove. I stored my pots on the stovetop, my pans in the oven and my dishes on the built-in shelves next to the fireplace in the library.

This was my first apartment living alone as I had always had roommates in Manhattan. I was close to thirty years old and at this point I was better off financially. I wasn't even close to getting married but decided it was time to settle down and make a home for myself. I wasn't waiting for any wedding shower to stock up so I bought twelve place settings plus the serving dishes and platters of the Wedgwood Green Chinese Tiger china pattern that I had wanted since I was ten years old; some nice linens and flatware from antique shows; professional grade stainless steel pots, pans, and cutlery; nested mixing bowls; measuring cups and spoons; and rubber spatulas. I also invested in an electric hand mixer and got rid of the manual eggbeater. Grandma Dexter had left me her crystal and several nice pieces of furniture. I supplemented the furniture with "family inventory" (affectionately called "FI" within the family. FI is crystal, silver, china or furniture, or even jewelry that belong to my parents but can go out on loan to the kids—sometimes indefinitely!).

Those were such memorable times and through *the tiny kitchen* I capture the special memories and share with you the recipes, menus and entertaining ideas. After surviving the tiny kitchens in Apartment 2C and on Prince Street, I vowed to write *the tiny kitchen*. It's now almost ten years later and I am now fulfilling that dream.

I have been married to my wonderful husband Bill for seven years. He loves cooking and entertaining as well and has contributed some of the recipes in this book. Although we have a much larger house now with a large modern kitchen and all the latest in kitchen gadgets and appliances, these recipes are near and dear to me. I still use them all on a regular basis (I still have a tiny kitchen mentality) and have shared many of them with my friends. They have all been time-tested and served on countless occasions.

the tiny kitchen is intended for all those who love to entertain and cook or aspire to do so. It doesn't matter if you live in an apartment, a townhouse or a single-family home. You may be a twenty-something just starting out in your own "Apartment 2C"; or you may have settled into a home that happens to have a tiny kitchen; or perhaps you have recently downsized from a big house with a spacious kitchen, or even if you just love to cook and entertain, *the tiny kitchen* is for you. Don't be intimidated by space limitations or resources. Be inventive and enjoy!

the tiny kitchen

the premise of this book is that space and, in many instances, time and supplies are at a premium. Anyone can whip up a fantastic meal or throw a great party when they have all the time in the world to prepare and a kitchen stocked with every gadget, spice, and flavored oil imaginable, and a fully outfitted kitchen with two ovens, warming drawers and an extra refrigerator for storage. Don't you love it when you watch a cooking show and they have each of the ingredients measured out in tiny glass bowls and displayed on the counter? Of course they have about 25-feet of counter space to work with. Who washes all those dishes anyway? Most people don't have these luxuries.

my tiny kitchen

I'm sharing with you the kitchen equipment and utensils I had on hand in my tiny kitchens. All recipes contained within *the tiny kitchen* can be made with the items on this list. Yes, you can make a great cake batter with a wooden spoon or a manual eggbeater—my grandmother did; and I did many times; it just takes a bit longer.

During my years in Manhattan I got by with just these items in my kitchen: 6-inch paring knife, 10-inch knife, potato peeler, wooden spoon, pastry blender, spatula (pancake turner), pastry brush, potato masher, tongs, hand eggbeater, rolling pin, small sieve, colander, garlic press, sifter, egg-slicer, cookie sheet, 4-sided grater, two 9-inch pie plates, a glass baking dish, jelly roll pan, roasting pan, a large and a small mixing bowl, a stock pot and two small sauce pans, a square baking pan, tube pan and large skillet.

Remember, I got these from Grandma Dexter's kitchen. To this day I still have them. The 4-sided grater still has the original price tag on; it cost 39 cents. I must admit, even to this day I've never used the egg-slicer, pastry blender or bread pan. The rolling pin, colander and sifter were original wedding gifts dating back to the 1920's and I am sure Grandma Dexter would get great pleasure in knowing they are still used regularly today.

what i wish i had

I had a glass in my cupboard that was just about a cup, or so it looked, so I used that for my measuring cup and did a lot of eyeballing. My flatware included a small spoon and a large spoon. I used the small one as a teaspoon and the large one as a tablespoon and improvised from there. I don't know why I didn't take the plunge and buy a measuring cup and measuring spoons; I guess I figured it made a good story that I was able to cook without them. But, there were some things that would have just plain made things easier. For about a $50.00 investment I could have had the things on this list that follows and still would have had plenty of storage room.

the well-stocked tiny kitchen

No matter how small your kitchen, you should be able to find room for these basic supplies. If necessary, store your pots on the stove top (they stack nicely inside each other) and your pans, pie plates, cookie sheet, cake rack and baking dishes in the oven like I did. I still store my roasting pans and broiler pan in the oven, for old times' sake. When using the oven or stove top, put the pots and pans you're not using on top of the refrigerator, a counter top, or stash them under a table somewhere until you're finished using their "home." The other supplies should fit into one cupboard and one drawer.

supplies

6-inch paring knife
10-inch knife
potato peeler
rubber spatula
pancake turner
sieve (*doubles as a sifter and colander*)
pastry brush
steamer (metal)
tongs
hand eggbeater
   (*can also be used to mash potatoes*)
rolling pin
2-cup glass measuring cup
set of measuring spoons

cake rack
cookie sheet
4-sided grater
two 9-inch pie plates
9 x 13-inch glass baking dish
jelly roll pan (14 ½ x 10 ½ x 1-inch)
roasting pan
broiler pan
nest of 4 glass mixing bowls
6-quart stock pot with lid
4-quart saucepan with lid
2-quart saucepan with lid
8 x 8-inch square baking pan
10-inch tube cake pan
10-inch skillet

If you have at least these things on hand you'll be golden. If you don't you might want to invest in what you don't have; I promise, you'll have room for all of it. If you have more than this, you have more than I did starting out.

prepared foods

Some foods are easier to buy prepared than make from scratch, and they are just as good as homemade. Some I always keep on hand and recommend in my recipes include: Newman's Own® Olive Oil and Vinegar Dressing; Newman's Own® Balsamic Vinaigrette; Swanson® Chicken Broth; Swanson® Beef Broth;

Pillsbury® Pie Crusts; McCormick® Sauce Blends (hollandaise, béarnaise, green peppercorn and hunter's); Pepperidge Farm® Puff Pastry Sheets; Pepperidge Farm® Patty Shells and Contadina® Pesto Sauce. (You probably have your own favorites, but these happen to be the ones I use regularly and always have in my cupboard).

You will see these called for in many recipes. If a recipe calls for chicken broth or beef broth, I suggest using Swanson®. The quality and flavor are very good. Feel free to use the low sodium versions if desired. Growing up, the only salad dressing I liked was my mother's oil and vinegar. We didn't use any bottled dressings until Newman's Own® came along. I use it religiously now for marinating chicken, beef, fish or lamb or as a salad dressing on green salads, pasta salad and wild rice salad and for coating potatoes. From time to time I will make my own dressing, but ninety-nine percent of the time, it's Newman's Own®.

There are some things you try once in your life, *and only once*. Making puff pastry from scratch was one of them—need I say more? Thank you Pepperidge Farm®!

Clockwise from upper right: Artichoke dip, raspberry brie, antipasto platter, tortellini with pesto dipping sauce.

Left to right: toffee bars, Billy's chili, the Senator's bourbon hot dogs.

Chocolate mousse in meringue nest.

Clockwise from top: Light nut bars, Grandma Dexter's pound cake, roasted turkey breast, overnight meringues, pumpkin chiffon pie, toffee bars, mince pie, cranberry-orange relish.

Gazpacho, tomato stuffed with chicken salad.

Pumpkin mousse.

Roasted garlic.

Brie with Prosciutto and ginger snaps.

the tiny kitchen

cooking and entertaining

appetizers

tortellini and pesto dipping sauce - 8

the senator's bourbon hot dogs - 9

sâté with three dipping sauces - 10

antipasto platter - 12

brie – three ways - 13

raspberry brie - 13

brie with prosciutto and ginger snaps - 14

pesto brie - 15

guacamole - 16

artichoke dip - 17

crispy southwestern roll-ups and avocado dip - 18

roasted garlic - 19

I am always in search of great easy-to-fix appetizers. I like the idea of always having a little something available for those spur-of-the-moment visitors or for the beginning of a great party. The roasted garlic is always a surprise treat for first time tasters. The first time we served this to my brother-in-law, Ted, and my nephew, Edward (who was only six at the time), they inhaled it and couldn't get enough. I encourage you to try it.

My favorite appetizer is the tortellini and pesto dipping sauce. There's a great story behind this. When I lived in Manhattan, my friend Sandy, who was getting married, invited me to accompany her to a cocktail reception for brides-to-be at Tiffany's. While she looked at silver, china, crystal and invitations, I followed the black-tied waiters around tasting the appetizers and champagne. One particular appetizer struck me as outstanding. On a silver tray were large tortellini skewered and a green sauce for dipping. I must have had at least a dozen. I didn't know what was in the sauce but it was delicious! For the next few days I couldn't stop thinking about the sauce and I was determined to re-create it. I'm not sure if I re-created it exactly, but what I came up with was a winner. When I served it to guests, they all wanted to know what was in the sauce. I've shared this with many of my friends and am always happy when they serve it.

An antipasto platter is plentiful enough for a meal. I first made it when I was going to a New Year's Eve Party at my sister Missy's house. About seven couples were contributing to the dinner party and each couple brought a course. Bill and I were responsible for the appetizer. I wanted something that I could prepare ahead of time, didn't need to be heated once I got there, and most importantly, something that was different—not just a standard cheese platter. I put this platter together and it was amazing how quickly it was eaten. I love putting this together because it's so beautiful and colorful and I get such pleasure out of everyone enjoying it. This platter was a huge hit and now I make it frequently for crowds.

tortellini and pesto dipping sauce

serves 6

1 package (9 ounces) tortellini
1 container (7 ounces) pesto sauce
1 container (16 ounces) sour cream
dash of salt
1 teaspoon olive oil

Fill a pot about two-thirds with water. Add salt and olive oil and bring to a boil.
Cook tortellini for about 7 minutes or until just tender. Be careful not to overcook the tortellini or the filling will start to come out.

   While the tortellini is cooking, make the sauce by mixing the pesto with the
sour cream until blended. Refrigerate for 1 - 2 hours. Bring to room temperature
before serving.

   Drain the tortellini and rinse with cold water and refrigerate.

---

serving suggestion

When ready to serve, fill a dish with pesto dip and place in the
middle of a plate or tray. Arrange the tortellini around the tray.
Serve with toothpicks.

   I have even served this with the tortellini right out of the boiling
water and the pesto sauce just made, however the pesto sauce
has a bit more flavor if it's refrigerated for about 1 - 2 hours first.

   I have also used the large tortellini and served them on skewers.
This looks really elegant, but is a lot of work for a large crowd.

---

the senator's bourbon hot dogs
serves 10

During my four years of college I was the perpetual intern for Lowell P. Weicker, Jr., U. S. Senator from Connecticut. He had an annual Christmas Party and made his famous bourbon hot dogs. To this day the Senator and I remain friends. I saw him the other day and told him I was writing a cookbook, so he gave me this recipe to share with you.

  1 package of hot dogs
  1 tablespoon butter
  1 bottle (14 ounces) ketchup
  1 cup bourbon
  4 tablespoons brown sugar

Cut each hot dog into bite-sized pieces. Melt the butter in a sauce pan and sauté the hot dog pieces for 2 - 3 minutes. Stir in the ketchup. Pour the bourbon into the empty ketchup bottle and swish around. Pour the bourbon on the hot dogs and add the brown sugar. Simmer uncovered for 10 minutes. Serve in a bowl with toothpicks.

sâté with three dipping sauces
serves 8 – 10

4 boneless chicken breasts
¾ cup Newman's Own® Olive Oil and Vinegar Dressing
Pesto Dipping Sauce (page 8)
Horseradish Sauce
Peanut Sauce

Cut the chicken into 1-inch cubes and marinate in the dressing for 30 minutes. Sauté the chicken over medium-high heat (add a bit of the dressing if necessary to keep the chicken from sticking) for about 10 minutes until done. Serve on a platter with dipping sauces using toothpicks or skewers.

horseradish sauce

½ cup mayonnaise
2 tablespoons horseradish (or to taste)
2 tablespoons sour cream
1 teaspoon minced shallots
Tabasco to taste

Mix all ingredients together in a small bowl. Refrigerate for 30 minutes.

peanut sauce

3 cups unsweetened coconut milk
¾ cup chunky peanut butter

⅓ cup brown sugar

⅓ cup soy sauce

1½ tablespoons rice vinegar

½ cup chopped scallions (green parts only)

2 tablespoons minced shallots

2 tablespoons minced garlic

¼ cup Thai red curry paste

1 teaspoon lime juice

2 cups chopped cilantro

⅓ cup finely minced basil

½ tablespoon cornstarch mixed with 1 tablespoon water

Place all ingredients except cornstarch in a saucepan. Stir constantly over medium-low heat just until the sauce begins to simmer but do not boil. Continue to cook, stirring frequently, until it thickens. If necessary to thicken more, combine ½ tablespoon of cornstarch with 1 tablespoon of water, stir to dissolve, and mix into the sauce until thoroughly combined; continue to cook until the sauce reaches the desired consistency. It should be fairly thick so it sticks to the chicken when dipped.

antipasto platter
serves 10

½ pound of each of the following sliced thin:
    Prosciutto, mortadello, pepperoni, hard salami, provolone cheese
¼ pound baby mozzarella balls (available in many gourmet shops)
¼ pound marinated mushrooms
1 jar (6 ounces) roasted red peppers slices
1 jar (12 ounces) peperoncini peppers in vinegar
1 jar (6 ounces) quartered and marinated artichoke hearts
½ pound mixed olives
sprigs of parsley, for garnish

Roll the individual slices of the meats and provolone cheese. I usually cut the provolone cheese in half, because it's too large to eat otherwise. Arrange the rolled meats on a plate or platter. Get creative—you can alternate them or put all of the same kind together. Decorate the platter with the rest of the ingredients in any order you like. Serve with fancy toothpicks.

brie three ways
serves 6

Lots of great cheeses are available today, but Brie is one of those old favorite standby cheeses that almost everyone likes. You can never go wrong with Brie—almost, that is. My first year in Manhattan my roommates Jenny, Moira, and I had a cocktail party. About an hour before the party, people started calling to ask if they could bring friends. We were now up to about eighty people and we had only prepared for fifty. So at the last minute I ran across the street and bought an 8-inch wheel of herbed Brie and more crackers. When I brought the Brie into the apartment Moira just about fainted from the smell of it. It was horrible and the entire apartment began to smell. I immediately opened the window (it was only about 30° outside), put the Brie on a plate and put it on the windowsill. The cold air masqueraded the rotten smell. From time to time I would glance at people tactfully spitting the Brie into their napkins. I honestly don't know if the Brie was rotten or if the herbs made it smell so, but to this day I never buy herbed Brie. Enjoy these three ways, they have always been a hit.

raspberry brie

> 1 wheel of Brie (8 ounces)
> 1 sheet puff pastry *(I prefer Pepperidge Farm®)*
> raspberry jam
> 1 egg, lightly beaten with 1 tablespoon cream

Thaw the puff pastry according to the directions on the package. Cut the sheet in half (that's enough for a small wheel of Brie) and roll out on a lightly floured surface into a 6 x 6-inch square. Cut a circle out of the pastry large enough to enclose the wheel of Brie. Spread the top and sides of the Brie with raspberry jam. Place the Brie top down into the center of the pastry. Fold the pastry over the Brie and fully enclose the Brie. Seal the seams by brushing with water and gently smoothing them. This may be prepared several hours in advance up to this point and refrigerated.

When ready to bake, preheat the oven to 400°. Place the Brie on an ungreased baking sheet seam side down and brush the top with egg wash. Bake for 30 minutes. Serve with thinly sliced French bread or assorted crackers.

brie with prosciutto and ginger snaps

This is a really interesting way to serve Brie. The salty Prosciutto, spicy ginger snaps, sweet apricots and creamy Brie make it a unique combination.

> 1 wedge of Brie at room temperature
> ½ pound Prosciutto
> dried apricots
> ginger snaps

Cut the Prosciutto crosswise into 2-inch pieces. Place the Brie and Prosciutto slices on a serving plate. Garnish the Brie with dried apricots. It's out of this world! Serve with ginger snaps.

pesto brie

> 1 wheel of Brie (8-ounces)
> 2 tablespoons pesto sauce
> 1 tablespoon pine nuts
> 1 roma tomato, seeded and chopped
> assorted crackers

Preheat the oven to 450°.

Trim the white skin off the top of the Brie. Spread pesto sauce on top of the Brie and sprinkle with pine nuts. Place in a pie plate and bake for 10 minutes.

Garnish with chopped tomatoes and serve warm with assorted crackers.

guacamole
serves 10 to 12

4 very ripe avocados
juice of 1 lemon or lime
10 dashes Tabasco
½ teaspoon salt
⅛ teaspoon cayenne pepper
2 roma tomatoes, seeded and diced
½ large red onion, diced
tortilla chips

Peel and pit the avocados and mash them in a mixing bowl with the lemon or lime juice. Leave some chunks—you don't want it like baby food Add salt, cayenne pepper and Tabasco and mix. Stir in the tomatoes and onions. If you do not plan to serve it immediately, cover with plastic wrap by placing the plastic wrap directly on the surface of the guacamole to keep the air from turning it brown. The flavor is enhanced if it is refrigerated for an hour. Serve with tortilla chips.

artichoke dip
serves 8

This recipe is so quick, easy and delicious. It's one I frequently prepare if friends just stop by. I have tried serving this with many different kinds of crackers and bread and always come back to the Pepperidge Farm® Butter Thins Crackers. They're in the shape of butterflies. It must be that their rich buttery flavor is enhanced by the ingredients in the dip.

    2 cans (14 ounces each) artichoke hearts
    1 cup mayonnaise
    1 cup sour cream
    ½ cup Parmesan cheese
    Pepperidge Farm® Butter Thins Crackers

Preheat the oven to 350°.

Chop the artichoke hearts coarsely. Mix together the mayonnaise, sour cream and Parmesan cheese. Add the chopped artichoke hearts and mix thoroughly. Pour into an ungreased 9-inch pie plate or other ovenproof baking dish. Bake for 20 minutes. Serve hot with Pepperidge Farm® Butter Thins Crackers.

crispy southwestern roll-ups and avocado dip
makes 1 dozen

12 medium flour tortillas
2 cups cooked, shredded chicken
1 jalapeno pepper, seeded and diced
1 red pepper, seeded and diced
1 cup cooked corn
½ cup diced red onion
2 tablespoons chopped fresh cilantro

juice of 1 lime
Tabasco to taste
1½ tablespoons cornstarch
1 cup shredded Monterey
   Jack cheese
¼ cup water
vegetable oil

Mix the chicken, peppers, corn, onion, cilantro, lime juice and Tabasco together. Blend together the cornstarch and water. Place chicken mixture and cheese on the left ⅓ of each tortilla. Brush the edges of the tortilla with the cornstarch mixture. Roll up the tortilla, tucking in the sides as you go along. It should look like an eggroll when it's rolled up. Pour enough vegetable oil in a stock pot so it is about 2 inches deep and heat over medium-high. It's hot enough when you drop a small piece of bread in it and it quickly turns brown. When the oil is hot enough cook the roll-ups for about 2 - 3 minutes until they are golden brown and crispy. Remove and drain on paper towel. To serve, slice in half on a diagonal. Serve warm.

avocado dip
makes about 1 cup

1 ripe avocado
1 teaspoon lime juice
2 tablespoons chopped cilantro
Tabasco to taste
1 teaspoon salt
½ cup sour cream
½ cup of milk or cream

Mash the avocado with a fork until smooth. Mix in lime juice, cilantro, Tabasco, salt, sour cream and milk until well blended. Serve immediately. This also goes well with Southwestern Chicken (page 42)

roasted garlic

serves 4

The first time I ever had roasted garlic was on our honeymoon. It seemed to be a popular item on the menu. Bill ordered it as an appetizer (against my best wishes) and when it was brought to the table it smelled so good it was irresistible. I think I ate more than he did. We had it a couple of more times that week. When we returned home I decided to put the garlic baker someone had given us for a gift to use. I urge you to try this!

1 head garlic
¼ teaspoon olive oil
¼ teaspoon thyme
salt and pepper to taste
wedge of saga cheese
1 baguette, sliced
4 sprigs of fresh parsley

> When roasted the garlic has a very creamy texture and a sweet, nutty flavor. It's very easy to remove and spread with a knife or cocktail fork. The combination of the garlic and the goat cheese makes for a very unique taste. The parsley is to be eaten afterward as it eliminates the garlic odor.

Preheat the oven to 350°.

Cut the tops (about ¼-inch) off the garlic to expose the cloves. Drizzle the garlic with olive oil and season with thyme, salt and pepper. Wrap the garlic loosely in tin foil, but be sure to close all the sides tightly (of course if you have a garlic baker, use that). Bake for 45 minutes. Place the garlic, cheese and baguette slices on a tray. Serve warm by spreading garlic, then goat cheese on baguette slices. Eat the parsley afterwards to freshen your breath.

salads

endive salad - 22

warm goat cheese salad - 23

tomato, basil and mozzarella salad - 24

wild rice salad - 25

pasta salad - 26

tabouleh - 27

brooklyn potato salad - 28

bill's cole slaw - 29

asian slaw - 30

hamptons seafood salad - 31

roasted chicken salad - 32

tomato stuffed with chicken salad - 33

Salads are great as a complement to a meal or as a meal in themselves. Growing up, salad consisted of cut up iceberg lettuce and peeled, sliced tomatoes (my mother and grandmother always peeled their tomatoes. When I started dabbling in the kitchen as a kid I did the same. It wasn't until I got much older that I realized peeling tomatoes was not the norm. It's pretty easy to do, however, using a paring knife). There were two choices of dressings: oil and vinegar or thousand island. Perhaps this was just my limited view and there was a whole world of salads I wasn't exposed to.

Over the years salads have been popularized by fresh produce sections of the store and salad bars carrying an endless variety of greens, fixings and dressings. Creativity is limited only to the imagination. Witness the variety of salad dressings available on grocery store shelves these days—Parmesan, ranch, honey mustard, Caesar, blue cheese, sun dried tomato, roasted garlic, raspberry walnut and the list goes on. My favorites are Newman's Own® Olive Oil and Vinegar and Newman's Own® Balsamic Vinaigrette. While I mention these in several recipes, feel free to substitute your own favorite dressing. Similarly, there are many great pre-packaged salad blends available: Italian, European, Mediterranean, Romaine, and American. Bill and I refer to these as "bag-o-salad." We use these almost exclusively as they are fresh and the work of washing, drying and tearing greens has been done.

The Hamptons seafood salad and chicken salad are meals in themselves. A buffet of a variety of salads makes a nice supper menu on a hot summer day.

endive salad

serves 4

This salad blends contrasting tastes and textures to create a wonderful combination. The endive's bitterness is balanced by the sweetness of the pear; the creamy cheese balanced by the crunchy walnuts.

2 heads Belgian endive, chopped
2 ounces saga cheese, crumbled
1 fresh pear, cored and diced
2 tablespoons chopped walnuts
¼ cup Newman's Own® Olive Oil and Vinegar Dressing

Toss all ingredients together gently and serve chilled.

warm goat cheese salad
serves 2

1 log (4 ounces) goat cheese
2 tablespoons breadcrumbs
cooking spray
2 cups of your favorite salad greens
Newman's Own® Balsamic Vinaigrette

Preheat the oven to 450°.

Slice the goat cheese in ½-inch slices. Coat each slice with breadcrumbs and lightly spray the tops with cooking spray. Place on a baking pan coated with cooking spray. Bake for 10 minutes. Serve on a bed of greens drizzled with vinaigrette.

tomato, basil and mozzarella salad

serves 2

1 large beefsteak tomato
1 ball fresh mozzarella
6 fresh basil leaves
fresh ground pepper
1 tablespoon olive oil

Slice the tomato and mozzarella into six slices each. Alternate slices of tomato, mozzarella and basil leaves on a plate. Season with pepper and drizzle with olive oil.

alternative serving suggestion

Try using grape or cherry tomatoes cut in half, chopped basil and either shredded mozzarella or baby mozzarella. Toss with the olive oil and pepper.

wild rice salad

serves 6

1 box (4 ounces) wild rice
2 ¾ cups chicken broth
½ cup diced celery
dash cayenne pepper
1 can (10.5 ounces) mandarin oranges
½ cup slivered almonds or chopped pecans
½ cup Newman's Own® Olive Oil Vinegar Dressing

Combine rice, chicken broth, celery and cayenne pepper in a saucepan. Bring to a boil. Reduce heat and simmer covered for 1 hour. Drain any liquid left in the pan. Let rice cool. Toss the rice, mandarin oranges, nuts and dressing together.

pasta salad

serves 6

This is a really pretty and colorful salad.

> 4 cups cooked bow tie pasta
> ½ red bell pepper, seeded and diced
> ½ yellow bell pepper, seeded and diced
> ¼ red onion, diced
> ½ cup chopped scallions (green parts only)
> 1 pint grape or cherry tomatoes, sliced in half
> ½ cup Newman's Own® Olive Oil and Vinegar Dressing

Toss all ingredients together. Serve chilled.

tabouleh

serves 4

I discovered tabouleh at a Lebanese restaurant. We were in a large group and I ordered it as an appetizer. It was so good I couldn't get enough of it. I thought for sure it was full of hidden calories but to my surprise it had almost no calories. It is a really nice refreshing salad. It's also nice served as an appetizer with pita bread.

 2 cups chopped fresh parsley
 ½ cup cooked couscous
 1 roma tomato, seeded and finely diced
 juice of 1 lemon
 1 tablespoon fresh chopped mint
 salt and pepper to taste

Mix all ingredients together and chill.

brooklyn potato salad
serves 8 - 10

There are many, many different varieties of potato salad. It seems everyone has their own secret ingredient and I'm not sure there are two alike. My mother learned to make potato salad from my Grandma Dexter and it's the only potato salad she really likes. When my mother tasted for the first time potato salad Bill had made she couldn't believe it —it was just like hers! When she told him, he told her he learned to make it from his mother. His mom was from Brooklyn as was Grandma Dexter. This must be the way they make potato salad in Brooklyn!

5 pounds white potatoes
1 cup diced celery
½ cup diced onions
2 large carrots, shredded
3 tablespoons chopped
    fresh parsley

2 cups mayonnaise
2 tablespoons celery seed
2 tablespoons sugar
¼ cup vinegar
salt and pepper to taste

Peel and quarter the potatoes and boil for 15 minutes or until fork tender. Drain and let cool for 30 minutes. Slice the potatoes in ⅛-inch slices into a large bowl. Add the celery, onions and carrots and mix gently. Mix the mayonnaise, celery seed, sugar, vinegar, salt and pepper in a small bowl. Add the mayonnaise mixture to the potato mixture. Mix thoroughly. For maximum flavor refrigerate for an hour before serving. Garnish with parsley.

bill's cole slaw
serves 6

My all time favorite cole slaw was the cole slaw that was served at Roy Rogers, which also happened to be my favorite fast-food restaurant. McDonald's bought out Roy Rogers several years ago and slowly converted the restaurants to McDonald's. The last Roy Rogers in my area was just closed a few weeks ago. No one's cole slaw could compare to Roy Rogers'. It was creamy, but not too mayonnaisey, not too wet, not too sweet and with the perfect balance of spices. Besides the mayonnaise the only ingredient I could identify was celery seed. I tried several times to duplicate their recipe with no success. The first time Bill made cole slaw I couldn't believe it. Bill's tasted just like Roy Rogers! Here it is...

4 cups shredded cabbage
2 large carrots, shredded
1½ cups mayonnaise
3 tablespoons cider vinegar
2 tablespoons celery seed
2 tablespoons sugar
salt and pepper to taste

In a large bowl combine cabbage and carrots. In a small bowl mix the mayonnaise, cider vinegar, celery seed, sugar, salt and pepper. Add the mayonnaise mixture to the cabbage mixture and mix thoroughly. Chill before serving.

asian slaw

serves 8

My friend Julie made this for a party and I must have had about five helpings. It was so good I just kept going back for more.

> 1 cup chopped almonds, roasted
> ½ cup sesame seeds, roasted
> 4 cups shredded cabbage
> 5 scallions, chopped (green parts only)
> ½ cup olive oil
> 6 tablespoons rice vinegar
> ⅛ teaspoon curry powder
> ¼ cup sugar
> 2 packages ramen noodles uncooked, broken into pieces

Preheat the oven to 350°.

Roast the almonds and sesame seeds for approximately 10 minutes. Turn frequently to prevent burning. Combine the cabbage and scallions in a large bowl. To make the dressing combine the olive oil, rice vinegar, curry powder and sugar in a small bowl and mix thoroughly. Add the dressing to the cabbage and mix thoroughly. Refrigerate for 2 - 3 hours. Mix in the roasted almonds, sesame seeds and ramen noodles just before serving.

hamptons seafood salad
serves 4

Bill and I were visiting my friend Cindy one weekend in the Hamptons. Bill ordered lobster salad one day for lunch and he thought he had died and gone to heaven. It looked so good I was dying to try it, but I am allergic to shellfish. When we got home I made this recipe and he loved it just as much as he had in the Hamptons. Buy the crabmeat, shrimp and lobster already cooked from your local market.

¼ red onion, finely diced
½ cup chopped scallions (green parts only)
½ cup celery, finely diced
1 cup cooked lump crabmeat
1 cup cooked lobster meat (¾-inch pieces)
1 cup cooked diced shrimp (¾-inch pieces)
1 cup mayonnaise
1 tablespoon lemon juice
1 tablespoon heavy cream (optional)
salt and pepper to taste

Mix the onion, scallions and celery in a medium bowl. Add the crabmeat, lobster meat and shrimp and toss gently to mix. In a small bowl mix the mayonnaise, lemon juice and cream. Season with salt and pepper. Add the mayonnaise to the seafood mixture and toss just enough to coat. Serve chilled on a bed of greens or on a small baguette or roll.

roasted chicken salad
serves 2

This makes a great meal from left over roasted chicken (page 45). Indulge and don't skimp on the dressing. Tossing everything together with the dressing makes it taste so much better than just drizzling the dressing on top.

3 cups of your favorite mixed greens
1 cup diced cooked chicken
½ cup cooked corn
¼ cup diced red onion
1 tomato, diced
½ avocado, diced
½ cup diced cucumber
½ cup shredded Monterey Jack cheese
¼ cup smoked almonds
½ cup Newman's Own® Olive Oil and Vinegar Dressing
½ cup croutons

Place all ingredients in a large bowl. Toss together to thoroughly coat the salad with dressing. Serve on chilled plates with crusty bread.

> Get creative with this salad. Don't worry if you don't have all these ingredients on hand. Use your imagination, if you have leftover vegetables like cooked asparagus, broccoli or green beans cut them into small bite sized pieces and add them. Also try crumbled bacon or diced red and green peppers or chopped scallions.

tomato stuffed with chicken salad
serves 4

Chicken salad has been one of my favorite salads for as long as I can remember. When my sister Missy was getting married, my sister Terry and I were hosting a bridesmaid luncheon for thirty. She and I were living in New York at the time. We drove with our friend Susie from New York to Virginia after work the night before the luncheon. By the time we finally started cooking it was about nine o'clock. The three of us stayed up until about one-o'clock in the morning making the chicken salad and preparing for the luncheon.

4 large tomatoes
2 cups cooked chicken cut in cubes
½ cup chopped celery
1 cup mayonnaise
¼ cup chopped parsley, dill, cilantro or tarragon
2 teaspoons capers
2 cups of your favorite mixed greens

Cut down each tomato in eighths not quite to the bottom. Combine chicken, celery, mayonnaise and parsley, dill, cilantro or tarragon. Place ½ cup of the chicken salad in each opened tomato. Top with ½ teaspoon of capers. Place on plate lined with your favorite greens. Garnish with hardboiled or deviled eggs and sliced hearts of palm.

poultry

coconut curry chicken - 36

creamed chicken with patty shells - 37

spicy chicken with bow tie pasta - 39

chicken in dry vermouth - 40

citrus chicken - 41

southwestern chicken - 42

raspberry chicken in puff pastry - 43

chicken with prosciutto and mozzarella - 44

roasted chicken – three ways - 45

old fashioned with brown gravy, with red wine, with white wine

cornish hen with wild rice - 48

cornish hen with orange sauce - 49

roasted turkey breast with cranberry orange-relish - 50

my absolute favorite poultry is a whole roasted chicken. I love it so much I have offered three different ways to prepare it: old fashioned, with white wine and herbs, and with red wine. I roast a whole chicken once a week, sometimes not for any particular meal but just to have around to nibble on. It makes the house smell so good while it's roasting and it reminds me of my grandmother's house. The crispy, seasoned skin of a roasted chicken just out of the oven is so tempting. Bill and I watch the clock for the obligatory five-minute cooling period for the bird to seal in the juices, then we make a mad dash and consume the skin before it starts to loose its crispness! Bill eats the wings immediately after the skin while I nibble on the leg and thigh as I make the gravy. I only acquired a true appreciation for dark meat a couple of years ago as I discovered its rich, moist distinctive flavor. It's so juicy and succulent. A lot of people don't care for it, and if you're one of those who haven't tried it from a freshly roasted chicken, I urge you to do so. You will become addicted! I usually serve roasted chicken with mashed potatoes, gravy and green beans. The leftover chicken goes in the refrigerator for sliced chicken sandwiches or reheated with leftover gravy and mashed potatoes.

I remember once I bought a hen that was on sale. I prepared it according to my old fashioned recipe. It smelled so good and the gravy was so rich and brown I couldn't wait to sink my teeth into it. But, to my surprise the meat was so tough we couldn't eat it. It was only later that my mother told me hens have been around the barnyard for a long time and are pretty old. If you do happen to get a hen, only use in a recipe that calls for stewing or cooking it very slowly for many hours — like my pulled chicken BBQ recipe (page 61).

coconut curry chicken
serves 4

This chicken has a little bit of a kick to it from the curry. It's colorful and delicious. To crisp up the coconut, just before taking the chicken out of the oven I turn the oven to broil for a minute or two.

4 boneless chicken breasts
4 tablespoons butter
½ cup honey
1½ tablespoons curry powder
1 tablespoon Dijon mustard
½ cup shredded coconut
½ cup heavy cream

Preheat the oven to 350°.

Melt the butter in a small saucepan over low heat. Add the honey, curry powder and Dijon mustard and mix. Place the chicken in a baking dish. Pour the honey mixture over the chicken breasts. Cover tightly with aluminum foil and bake covered for 20 minutes. Sprinkle the coconut over the chicken and bake uncovered for an additional 15 minutes. Remove the chicken from the pan and set aside covered. Add the heavy cream to the pan juices and cook over medium heat on the stovetop until just thickened. Serve chicken over steamed basmati rice (page 88) and gingered carrots (page 93) on the side.

creamed chicken with patty shells

serves 6

This dish is a real crowd pleaser. It's filling, and inexpensive. My mother made it for years for her dinner parties. We served this at the first dinner party my sister Terry and I had on our own during our college years. The nice thing about it is you can serve it to a crowd and if you don't have enough seats at a table for your guests, it's easy to eat from a plate on your lap. For the cooked chicken I usually simmer breasts in broth for about 30 minutes.

½ cup butter
½ cup flour
2 cups chicken broth
¾ teaspoon salt
¾ cup light cream
3 cups cut-up cooked chicken, preferably white meat
1 package frozen patty shells *(I prefer Pepperidge Farm®)*
1½ cups cooked broccoli florets

Cook the patty shells according to the directions on the package. Melt the butter in a large saucepan over low heat. Add the flour and cook, stirring constantly until it begins to bubble. *Do not let it brown!* Remove from heat and gradually whisk in the chicken broth stirring constantly. Add the salt and cream. Cook over medium heat stirring constantly (being careful not to let it boil) until the sauce has thickened. If you are not ready to serve at this point, remove it from the heat.

Once ready to serve, add the chicken to the sauce heating through. Stir gently so chicken doesn't stick to the bottom of the pan. You do not want the chicken to be in the sauce too long as it will begin to shred and will overcook becoming tough and stringy. Fill the patty shells with the creamed chicken and let the sauce drip over the sides. Serve with steamed broccoli (page 90) on the side.

variations

You can mix the broccoli into the cream sauce adding it after the chicken. You may also substitute peas, asparagus, carrots or vegetables of choice for the broccoli.

For those who may be lactose intolerant or prefer a lighter sauce use all stock instead of chicken stock and cream. It's just as delicious.

spicy chicken with bow tie pasta

serves 4

4 boneless chicken breasts
4 tablespoons blackening seasoning
1 tablespoon Hungarian paprika
dash of cayenne pepper
1 teaspoon dried thyme
3 tablespoons olive oil
½ cup white wine
1 cup chicken broth
4 cups cooked bow tie pasta

> This chicken is a bit spicy. To make it milder, eliminate the cayenne pepper, decrease the amount of blackening seasoning and increase the amount of paprika used.

Cut the chicken into 1½-inch cubes. Mix the blackening seasoning, paprika, cayenne pepper and thyme together in a large bowl. Toss the chicken in the seasoning to coat. Heat olive oil over high heat in a large sauté pan and sear the chicken on all sides (about 5 minutes). Remove the chicken from the pan, add the white wine and any leftover seasoning mix and deglaze the pan. Cook stirring constantly for 1 - 2 minutes. Stir in the chicken broth. Return the chicken to the pan and simmer covered for about 10 minutes to finish cooking the chicken. Remove the chicken from the pan with a slotted spoon and bring the sauce to a boil for 1 - 2 minutes to thicken. Return the chicken to the pan. Place the pasta in four pasta bowls; spoon chicken and sauce over the pasta.

chicken in dry vermouth

serves 4

4 boneless chicken breasts
2 tablespoons olive oil
1 shallot, diced
½ cup diced baby carrots
½ cup diced celery
½ cup dry vermouth or other dry white wine
½ cup chicken broth
salt and pepper to taste
2 cups cooked couscous (page 87)

Heat the olive oil in a sauté pan over medium high heat. Sauté the shallot, carrots and celery for 1 - 3 minutes. Add the chicken and sauté together for 5 minutes, turning once. Add the vermouth and chicken broth. Reduce heat and simmer covered for 20 minutes or until done.

Remove the chicken and keep warm by covering with foil. With the vegetables still in the pan reduce the liquid until it begins to thicken slightly. Season to taste. Serve the chicken over a bed of couscous, and top the chicken with the sauce and vegetables.

citrus chicken
serves 4

My friend Moira and I were having a going away party for about thirty people for our friend Jenny who was moving to South Carolina. We had it at Moira's parents' apartment, which had a tiny kitchen. The night before the party we were making up these foil packets in the living room. We opened a bottle of wine, created an assembly line and made those packets in no time at all. What great fun! Cooking in the foil packet creates its own juice, which makes a nice sauce by itself.

    4 boneless chicken breasts
    2 tablespoons chopped parsley
    2 tablespoons chopped dill
    1 teaspoon chopped mint
    1 lemon sliced into ¼-inch slices
    1 lime sliced into ¼-inch slices

Preheat the oven to 375°.

  Mix the parsley, dill and mint together in a small bowl. Cut four pieces of aluminum foil approximately 12 inches long. Place a chicken breast in the middle of each piece of foil and top with the herb mixture, then place a lemon and lime slice on top. Create foil packets by bringing the ends of the foil together and rolling down and fold the sides up. Place on a shallow baking dish. Bake for approximately 30 minutes.

southwestern chicken

serves 4

4 boneless chicken breasts
1 package taco seasoning mix
1 jalapeno pepper, seeded and diced
1 red pepper, seeded and diced
1 cup cooked corn
½ cup diced red onion
2 tablespoons cilantro
juice of 1 lime
several dashes Tabasco

Preheat the oven to 375°.

Rinse the chicken and coat it with the taco seasoning mix. Cut four pieces of aluminum foil about 12 inches each. Mix the diced peppers, corn, red onion, cilantro, lime juice and Tabasco together in a bowl. Place a chicken breast in the middle of each piece of foil. Top each chicken breast with ¼ cup of the mixture. Create foil packets by joining the two opposite ends in the middle and folding down. Fold the sides of the foil packets so there are no openings. Place on a jelly roll pan. Bake for 30 minutes. Serve with Spanish Rice (page 88)

---

southwestern potatoes

Serving new red potatoes dusted with the remaining taco seasoning mix is a nice alternative to the Spanish rice. Cut the potatoes in half or quarters. Boil for 8 minutes. Drain and let cool. Coat the potatoes with the excess taco seasoning mix. Use olive oil to coat the bottom of a baking dish. Place the potatoes in the dish and bake at the same time as the chicken for 30 minutes.

raspberry chicken in puff pastry

serves 4

4 boneless chicken breasts
1 wheel Brie (8 ounces), skin removed
½ cup high quality raspberry jam (without seeds, if possible)
1 sheet of puff pastry *(I prefer Pepperidge Farm®)*
1 egg, lightly beaten with 1 tablespoon cream

Preheat the oven to 375°.

Bring the puff pastry to room temperature and roll out on a floured surface into a 12 x 14-inch rectangle. Cut the pastry into four rectangular pieces large enough to wrap each chicken breast. Cut the Brie into 8 slices. Spread raspberry jam in the center of each piece of puff pastry and top with slices of Brie. Place the chicken in the center of the puff pastry on top of the Brie. Fold the edges of the puff pastry over the chicken to fully enclose, cutting off any excess pastry. Brush the seams of the puff pastry with water to seal. You want the chicken to be completely wrapped in the puff pastry with no holes or open seams where juices will escape. Place the chicken in a baking dish and brush with the egg wash. Bake for 30 minutes.

> These may be made ahead of time and frozen. If you plan to make ahead and freeze, brush with the egg wash just before baking and bake at 375° for 40 minutes.

prosciutto and mozzarella chicken

serves 4

4 chicken breasts
2 tablespoons olive oil
1 clove garlic, minced
1 cup chicken broth
4 ounces Prosciutto
4 ounces mozzarella
2 tablespoons fresh chopped basil

Heat the olive oil in a sauté pan over medium high heat. Add garlic and sauté for 2 - 3 minutes. Add the chicken and sauté together for 5 minutes, turning once. Add the chicken broth, reduce heat and simmer covered for 10 minutes. Top each chicken breast with a slice of Prosciutto then mozzarella. Continue to simmer covered for 10 minutes. Place each chicken breast on a plate and top with fresh basil. Serve with a side of pesto penne (page 80).

roasted chicken - three ways
serves 4

old fashioned with brown gravy

>   1 roasting chicken (4 - 6 pounds)
>   2 large carrots cut into large pieces or several baby carrots
>   1 onion, quartered
>   2 stalks celery cut into large pieces
>   salt and pepper to taste
>   2 cups canned chicken broth
>   chicken stock from giblets
>   ½ cup flour

Preheat the oven to 350°.

Remove the giblets and rinse the cavity of the chicken. Put the giblets in 4 - quart pot filled with water. Add half of the carrots, onion and celery. Bring to a boil, then simmer covered for about an hour.

Meanwhile season the chicken with salt and pepper and place in a roasting pan. Add the remaining carrots, onions and celery. Pour 1 cup of chicken broth into the roasting pan. Roast for 20 - 25 minutes per pound, basting every 15 minutes (adding more chicken broth if necessary). To test whether it's done, pierce the thigh with the tip of a knife. If clear juices run out, it's done. Some birds have a built in timer to indicate when it's done; they are very accurate.

When the giblets have finished cooking, discard them (or cut up and put in the gravy, if you like) and the vegetables. You have a nice rich stock to use in making the gravy. When the chicken has finished roasting, place on a cutting board and let cool while making the gravy.

Place the roasting pan on the stove top. Remove all but about three table-spoons of fat from the pan. Add about ½ cup of homemade chicken stock and deglaze the pan scraping up the brown pieces. Stir in the flour until it's well blended. Add 1 cup of chicken stock and blend in, over medium heat, stirring constantly until the gravy thickens. If it becomes too thick add more stock until it's the consistency you like. Adjust the seasoning with salt. Slice the chicken and serve with old-fashioned mashed potatoes (page 86) smothered in gravy; steamed carrots (page 90) and cranberry-orange relish (page 51).

roasted chicken with red wine reduction

> 1 roasting chicken (4 - 6 pounds)
> 3 tablespoons chopped fresh rosemary
> salt and pepper to taste
> 2 cups chicken broth
> 1½ cups dry red wine

Preheat the oven to 350°.

Remove the giblets and discard. Season the chicken with salt, pepper and rose-mary and place in a roasting pan. Pour 1 cup of chicken broth and ½ cup red wine in the roasting pan. Roast for 20 - 25 minutes per pound, basting every 15 minutes (adding more chicken broth if necessary). To test whether it's done, pierce the thigh with the tip of a knife. If clear juices run out, it's done. Some birds have a built in timer to indicate when it's done; it is very accurate.

When the chicken has finished roasting, place on a cutting board and let cool while making the gravy. Skim the fat from the pan just leaving the juices. Add 1 cup of red wine and deglaze the pan scraping up the brown pieces. Reduce the sauce until it's the consistency you like. Adjust the seasoning with salt. Slice the chicken and serve with wild rice and spoon the sauce over top.

chicken with white wine reduction

Prepare chicken as above but eliminate the rosemary and substitute dry white wine for the red wine to make the sauce. Rub the chicken with a garlic clove, then the juice of one lemon. Season with salt and pepper. Roast according to the above instructions. This has a much lighter flavor than with the red wine or the brown gravy.

---

roasted chicken and pesto sandwiches

Leftover roasted chicken sliced makes a great sandwich. I often make these sandwiches for a picnic dinner for outdoor concerts in the park at Wolf Trap.

1 fresh baguette
sliced white meat chicken
2 roma tomatoes, sliced
Pesto Dipping Sauce (page 8)
fresh mozzarella, sliced

Slice the baguette lengthwise. Spread pesto dipping sauce on the inside top and bottom of the sliced baguette. Place a layer of chicken on the bottom half of the baguette; top with a layer of tomatoes then a layer of mozzarella. Put the top on the baguette. Slice baguette into 2 inch slices.

---

cornish hen and wild rice
serves 4

This is a recipe my mother used to make for dinner parties. She would cut each hen in half and serve on a silver tray with a bed of wild rice. My father likes to tell the story of the time when one of their dinner party guests cut into their hen and it went flying off the dinner plate. My mother tells the story of the same dinner party where she asked my dad, who was in the kitchen, to check on the hens in the oven. His response was, "Sure dear. Where is the oven?"

    4 Cornish hens
    ¾ cup dry red wine
    ¾ cup chicken broth
    ½ cup sour cream
    ½ cup sliced mushrooms, sautéed lightly
    2 cups cooked wild rice (page 87)

Preheat the oven to 425°.

Remove the giblets from the hens and rinse the cavities. Put the hens in a roasting pan and pour the wine and broth over the birds. Bake for 45 - 60 minutes, basting every 15 minutes. If needed add more broth to the pan. Remove hens from the pan and keep warm. Place the pan on the stove top over medium-high heat and reduce the liquid. Stir in the sour cream but do not let boil. Add mushrooms. Serve hens cut in half with wild rice and spoon the sauce over it; accompany with steamed asparagus (page 90).

cornish hen with orange sauce
serves 4

4 Cornish hens
1 orange, quartered
1 cup orange juice
½ cup dry white wine
½ cup orange marmalade
10 ounce can mandarin oranges, drained or ½ orange sliced thin

Preheat the oven to 425°.

Rinse the cavities of the hens and place ¼ orange in each. Put the hens in a roasting pan and pour the orange juice and wine over the birds. Bake for 45 - 60 minutes, basting every 15 minutes. If needed, add more orange juice or some water to the pan. Remove hens from the pan and keep warm. Place the pan on the stove top over medium-high heat and reduce the liquid, stir in the marmalade and add the mandarin oranges or orange slices. Serve with the sauce spooned over the hens and accompany with basmati rice (page 88), gingered carrots (page 93) and cranberry-orange relish (page 51).

Pull any leftover hen from the bones and add it along with any leftover sauce to some cooked wild rice to make a wonderful second meal. Serve it either warm or cold with a great green salad, fruit, cheese and French bread.

roasted turkey breast
serves 6

Roasted turkey breasts are a great alternative to a whole turkey, especially if you have a small oven or minimal room in the refrigerator. One turkey breast will feed about six.

     1 fresh turkey breast (5 - 7 pounds)
     salt and pepper to taste
     4 tablespoons butter, melted
     4 cups chicken broth
     3 tablespoons flour

Preheat the oven to 350°.

Rinse the turkey and pat dry. Season with salt and pepper. Brush the top of the turkey with melted butter. Place in a roasting pan and pour in 1 cup of the chicken broth. Roast for 15 - 20 minutes per pound, basting every 20 minutes adding more chicken broth if necessary. Once the turkey is done, remove the breast to a cutting board and let cool while making the gravy. For easier carving let cool at least 20 minutes.

Place the roasting pan on the stove top. Remove all but about three tablespoons of fat from the pan. Add about ½ cup of chicken broth and deglaze the pan scraping up the brown pieces. Remove from heat and stir in the flour until it's well blended and there are no lumps. Adding flour over heat causes lumps. Once the flour is well blended add 2 cups of broth and heat the gravy over medium heat stirring constantly until the gravy thickens. If it becomes too thick add more broth until it's the consistency you like. Adjust the seasoning with salt. Serve the turkey breast sliced with hot gravy, mashed potatoes and green peas.

cranberry-orange relish

1 pound cranberries
1 cup water
2 apples, peeled and diced
1 cup peeled and diced orange
3 ½ cups sugar
zest of 1 orange (optional)
½ cup chopped pecans

Wash the cranberries. Place in a large saucepan and cover with water. Bring to a boil and simmer until berries pop. Add apples, oranges, sugar and orange zest. Cook over medium heat, stirring occasionally until thick, approximately 30 minutes. Remove from heat and add pecans. Pour into a bowl and refrigerate for 2 hours.

meat

whole roasted beef tenderloin - 54

broiled filet mignon with sautéed mushrooms - 55

beef wellington - 56

beef stroganoff - 57

breaded pork chops - 58

pork tenderloin - 60

pulled pork bbq (or chicken or beef) - 61

broiled balsamic lamb chops - 62

leg of lamb with roasted potatoes - 63

veal with artichokes - 65

growing up we ate a lot of meat, particularly beef and lamb, which my mother prepared regularly, and on occasion we'd have a veal dish. Sundays we'd have either steak and baked or mashed potatoes or roasted leg of lamb with roasted potatoes and gravy. We didn't eat much pork, however I have come to fix it frequently in recent years. I'm not sure if it's due to the persuasive power of the Pork Council's advertising campaign—"pork, the other white meat" or the fact that Bill really likes it. Pork tenderloins are very moist and tender as are pork loin chops, if they're not overcooked.

It's important to get a good quality cut of meat or else it's going to be tough and stringy. If you are unsure what defines good quality, ask your butcher what the best cut will be for what you're going to prepare. I appreciate each kind of meat for its distinctive flavor.

I've included some quick, easy-to-prepare recipes for when cooking and preparation time are at a minimum—broiled filet mignon, balsamic lamb chops and pork tenderloin. Coupled with steamed vegetables you have a meal in a matter of minutes.

whole roasted beef tenderloin
serves 6 - 8

You can't go wrong with serving beef tenderloin. It's such a flavorful, tender cut of meat that requires little preparation or cooking time. Even though it's a bit more expensive than other cuts of beef, it's well worth it. I offer three of my favorite ways to serve it.

> 1 whole beef tenderloin (6 - 7 pounds)
> Newman's Own® Olive Oil and Vinegar Dressing
> salt and pepper, to taste
> McCormick® Béarnaise Sauce Mix

Preheat the oven to 425°.

Trim the tenderloin of excess fat and scrappy ends and remove the thin silvery membrane. Brush the tenderloin with the dressing, season with salt and freshly ground black pepper. Put the tenderloin in a roasting pan and roast 30 minutes for rare and 40 minutes for medium-rare.

Prepare béarnaise sauce mix according to the directions on the package. Serve tenderloin sliced with the sauce and assorted steamed vegetables.

> ### sliced tenderloin
>
> After roasting the tenderloin let it cool completely. Slice thinly for a cocktail buffet.

broiled filet mignon with sautéed mushrooms
serves 2

This is a great alternative to a whole beef tenderloin if you're just having dinner for a two.

> 2 filet mignons (1½ -inches thick)
> salt and pepper to taste
> 2 tablespoons butter
> ¾ cup sliced white mushrooms
> ¼ cup dry red wine
> 1 package McCormick® Green Peppercorn Sauce

Preheat the broiler.

Season the meat with salt and pepper. Place on a broiler pan and broil for 5 minutes per side for rare and 7 - 9 minutes per side for medium.

While the meat is cooking melt the butter in a sauté pan over medium heat. Add the mushrooms and sauté for 2 - 3 minutes. Add the red wine and simmer while the meat is broiling. Prepare the green peppercorn sauce mix according to the instructions on the package. Serve the filet topped with the sautéed mushrooms and sauce.

beef wellington
serves 8

1 whole beef tenderloin (6 - 7 pounds)
Newman's Own® Olive Oil and Vinegar Dressing
salt and pepper to taste
1 slice (1½-inch) truffle mousse pâté, softened
1 sheet puff pastry *(I prefer Pepperidge Farm®)*
1 egg, lightly beaten with 1 tablespoon cream

Preheat the oven to 425°.

Trim the tenderloin of excess fat and scrappy ends and remove the thin silvery membrane. Brush with dressing; season with salt and pepper. Roast according to the recipe on page 54. Let the tenderloin cool completely (you may want to cook it the day before). Spread the pâté over the top and sides of the cooled tenderloin. Roll out the puff pastry to a 12 x 14-inch rectangle. Place the tenderloin in the middle of the puff pastry, top side down and fold the edges over the tenderloin so it is fully enclosed. Seal the seams of the puff pastry by brushing it with water. Preheat the oven to 425°. Place the filet in a roasting pan, seam side down. Brush top and sides with the egg wash and bake for 25 minutes. Cut into 1-thick slices.

madeira sauce

This is a rich sauce that compliments the beef wellington.

3 tablespoons butter
3 tablespoons minced shallots
½ cup Madeira
1½ cups beef broth
1 tablespoon cornstarch
2 teaspoons cold water

Melt the butter in a small saucepan. Add the shallots and cook until tender. Add the Madeira and beef broth. Simmer for 5 minutes. Mix the cornstarch with the water. Whisk into the sauce and simmer another 15 minutes.

beef stroganoff

serves 6

2 pounds sirloin steak, cut into thin 1 x 1½-inch strips
6 tablespoons butter
½ medium onion, minced
½ cup sliced mushrooms
salt and pepper to taste
⅛ teaspoon nutmeg
2 teaspoons paprika
¼ cup beef broth
1 cup sour cream
1 package (12 ounces) egg noodles, cooked

Over medium-high heat melt 3 tablespoons of the butter in a large sauté pan and sauté the onions until tender, about 1 - 2 minutes. Remove and set aside. Over medium-high heat add the meat and brown on all sides. Remove and set aside. Keeping the juices in the pan add the remaining 3 tablespoons of butter and add the mushrooms and cook over medium heat for 2 minutes. Add the salt, pepper, nutmeg, paprika and beef broth. Lower the heat and whisk in the sour cream. Return the beef and onions to the pan and heat through. Do not let the sauce boil. Serve the stroganoff over the cooked noodles.

breaded pork chops

serves 4

4 pork chops (1-inch thick)
1 egg
3 tablespoons milk
¾ cup breadcrumbs
1 tablespoon Italian seasoning
½ teaspoon garlic powder
½ teaspoon onion powder
⅛ teaspoon sage
¼ teaspoon oregano
⅛ teaspoon salt
dash pepper
¼ cup olive oil
1 can (14.5 ounces) sauerkraut
1 jar (24 ounces) applesauce

Preheat the oven to 350°.

Trim the pork chops of any excess fat. Beat the egg and milk together until thoroughly mixed. Blend together the breadcrumbs, Italian seasoning, garlic powder, onion powder, sage, oregano and salt and pepper

Dip the pork chops in the egg mixture and coat thoroughly. Then dip into the bread crumb mixture and coat liberally and set aside on a plate. Heat the oil over medium high heat in a large sauté pan. Place the pork chops in the pan and cook for about 3 minutes on each side until the breadcrumbs have formed a nice brown crust. Remove from the sauté pan and place on a broiler pan. Bake for 25 minutes. Serve with steamed broccoli (page 90), applesauce, and sauerkraut and lumpy red mashed potatoes (page 86).

substitutions

You can buy Italian style breadcrumbs and eliminate all the spices if you don't have them on hand or you can use just the plain breadcrumbs.

If you don't have a broiler pan you can bake in a baking dish. The broiler pan lets the juices drip down and keeps the coating crispy.

pork tenderloin
serves 4

I've included this pork tenderloin recipe because pork is often overlooked as an entrée. It is a great alternative to chicken and beef. The tender texture and moistness makes it melt in your mouth. It's easy to fix, and requires minimal preparation. I have bought both plain and preseasoned—pepper crusted, and lemon-herb. They're all good.

> 1 boneless pork tenderloin (1-2 pounds)
> salt and pepper to taste
> 1 package McCormick® Green Peppercorn Sauce

Preheat the oven to 350°.

Season the tenderloin with salt and pepper and place in a roasting pan. Roast for 40 minutes. Let cool for 5 minutes before slicing. While cooling, prepare the peppercorn sauce according to the directions on the package adding the juices from the roasting pan. Serve with spiced creamy potatoes (page 85).

pulled pork bbq (or chicken or beef)

serves 10

4 pounds pork roast
1 can (29 ounces) tomato sauce
3 large onions chopped
4 garlic buds chopped
½ cup brown sugar
½ cup cider vinegar
½ cup soy sauce
Worcestershire sauce to taste
Tabasco to taste
salt and pepper to taste

I usually take two days to make this. After the meat has finished cooking I remove it and put it in a bowl in the refrigerator. I pour the sauce into a pitcher and refrigerate. The next day I skim the fat from the surface of the sauce before cooking it down.

This recipe is just as good made with beef brisket or a whole roasting chicken. This makes a lot, but it freezes very well and can easily be thawed and reheated.

In a large stockpot combine all the ingredients *except* the pork. Mix together thoroughly. Add the pork and bring to a boil. Lower the heat and simmer covered for about 6 hours. The meat will become very, very tender.

Remove the meat from the sauce and let cool until it's cool to the touch. Pull the meat apart into bite sized pieces and place in a separate bowl. Boil the sauce down until it's a nice thick consistency (not runny). Re-season the sauce to taste if necessary. Put the meat back into the sauce and mix thoroughly until the meat is coated.

Serve on sesame seeded hamburger buns with Bill's coleslaw (page 29).

broiled balsamic lamb chops

serves 2

Lamb is traditionally served with mint jelly or a mint sauce. Try it with the rich hunter sauce, it gives it a very different flavor.

    4 lamb chops about 1½-inches thick
    Newman's Own® Balsamic Vinaigrette
    1 package McCormick® Hunter Sauce Mix

Brush the lamb chops with the vinaigrette. Place in a broiler pan and place under the broiler. Broil for 5 minutes on each side for pink or 8 minutes on each side for more well done.

Prepare the hunter sauce mix according to the directions on the package. Serve with sea salt roasted potatoes (page 84) and steamed green beans (page 90).

leg of lamb with roasted potatoes
serves 6

my father absolutely loves roasted leg of lamb. As a child he grew up on it as Grandma Sullivan frequently made it for the Sullivan Family Sunday afternoon suppers in the Bronx. My father tells a great story of those Sundays. All the relatives would congregate at their apartment; women in the kitchen preparing a feast and the men in the living room having a scotch or two and lots of laughs. After dinner Irish tempers would flair and everyone would storm off mad. But, they'd be back again the following Sunday forgetting about the fights and sharing another Sunday supper in the Bronx.

For years he requested this meal for his Father's Day and birthday dinners. One year we decided to get him a smoker for Father's Day and smoke the leg of lamb. This was the first time any of us had ever used a smoker. My father was skeptical of the smoker and just wanted the lamb roasted like my mother had done for years. We insisted on smoking it. After an hour of smoking my brother Robert checked on the lamb and it wasn't anywhere near being done. He made a few adjustments to the smoker and checked on it again thirty minutes later. He came back in the house with his eyebrows singed and announced we now had blackened leg of lamb. It was burnt to a crisp and inedible. My father got the pleasure of an "I told you so" and then we went out to dinner. The following week my father gave the smoker away.

  1 whole bone-in leg of lamb (4 - 5 pounds)
  1 peeled large carrot cut into 2 - 3 pieces or 6 baby carrots

1 onion cut in quarters
6 large russet potatoes, peeled and quartered
salt and pepper to taste

for the gravy

½ cup red or white wine, optional

water

½ cup of flour

Preheat the oven to 450°.

Season the lamb with salt and pepper. Place carrots, onion and leg of lamb in a roasting pan. Roast for 10 - 15 minutes. Add the potatoes, coating them with the fat that has accumulated in the bottom of the pan. Reduce the heat to 350° and roast for 15 - 18 minutes per pound. If you're using a meat thermometer, the lamb will be cooked rare at 130° - 135°.

Transfer the potatoes to a smaller pan and put back in the oven (turned off) to keep warm. Transfer the lamb to a cutting board. Discard the onion. Skim off all but 3 tablespoons of fat from the pan. Transfer the roasting pan to the stove top and over medium-high heat, deglaze the pan with the wine or if you choose not to use wine, deglaze with ½ cup of water. Mash the carrots as you deglaze the pan by pressing down with the back of a spoon. Remove the pan from the heat after deglazing and quickly whisk in flour. Cook for 3 - 5 minutes over medium heat. Gradually add approximately 1½ - 2 cups of water stirring constantly over medium heat until thickened. Add more water if the gravy is thicker than you like. Season with salt and pepper. Pour juices that have accumulated on the cutting board or those that accumulate as the lamb is carved into the gravy. Serve with Grandma Sullivan's rutabaga (page 91) and Harvard beets (page 92) on a chilly Sunday afternoon.

veal with artichokes

serves 4

1 pound veal scallopini
3 tablespoons flour
¼ teaspoon salt
¼ teaspoon pepper
2 tablespoons butter
2 tablespoons shallots, minced
juice of 1 lemon
½ cup dry white wine
1 can (14 ounces) artichoke hearts, quartered
1 tablespoon capers

Combine flour, salt and pepper. Coat the veal with the flour mixture and set aside. Melt the butter in a sauté pan over medium-high heat. Add the veal and quickly brown on both sides. Remove veal from the pan and set aside. Add lemon juice and wine and deglaze the pan. Stir in artichokes and capers and cook over high heat until the liquid is reduced and slightly thickened. Return the veal to the pan and heat through. Serve with a side of pesto penne (page 80).

fish

not

in

the

tiny

kitchen.

it

smells.

soups, stews and pastas

consommé - 70

tortilla soup - 71

chicken noodle soup - 72

gazpacho - 73

billy's chili - 74

jambalaya - 76

scotch broth - 77

beef burgundy - 78

pasta bolognese - 79

pesto penne - 80

asparagus risotto - 81

every year I anxiously await the change of seasons from summer to autumn. It seems there's that one pivotal day when you wake up and there's a chill in the air. It's time to pull out the turtlenecks, sweaters, jackets and socks. The crisp air gives me a feeling of freedom and happiness. It's my favorite time of year and I feel an excitement as I think about wood burning fires and the upcoming holidays. The weather encourages homey, comfort foods. This day seems to always fall on a Sunday and I herald the changing seasons by spending the afternoon in the kitchen preparing a yummy and appropriately hearty early supper. The aroma of gently simmering beef burgundy fills the air, as does the sweet and spicy aroma of Grandma Dexter's apple pie. Fresh hot crusty bread with soft butter and a good bottle of red wine transforms beef burgundy into a rustic meal. I'm ready to settle in for the winter ahead and count the days until I can start playing Christmas carols.

You will find each of the selections in this chapter equally satisfying and abundant for a mid-winter's meal.

consommé
serves 4

We had received some elegant soup bowls for a wedding gift, and my husband had given me some soup spoons to our sterling flatware as a birthday present. The year we were married, I invited my parents over for Thanksgiving dinner. I started with this soup as the first course. My only purpose in having soup with the meal was to be able to use the elegant new soup bowls and sterling soup spoons. I didn't want a heavy soup and knew my parents both liked consommé. I didn't have any intentions of making it from scratch, so I added the red wine and Cognac to the beef broth, and the scallions and just 2 - 3 tortellini per bowl for a touch of elegance. My parents loved it and thought it was homemade!

    3 cups beef broth
    ½ cup dry red wine
    1 tablespoon Cognac
    ½ cup chopped scallions, green parts only
    1 package cheese tortellini

Cook tortellini according to directions on the package. In a saucepan bring the beef broth, red wine and cognac to a boil. Reduce heat and simmer for 15 minutes. Add scallions and the cooked tortellini just before serving.

tortilla soup

serves 8

2 tablespoons olive oil
1 large onion, chopped
2 garlic cloves, minced
¼ cup chopped cilantro
½ teaspoon cumin
2 jalapeno peppers, finely diced
2 scallions, chopped, green and white parts
5 cups chicken broth
2 cups diced *cooked* chicken or turkey
1 cup cooked corn
2 roma tomatoes, seeded and chopped
8 ounces shredded cheddar cheese
1 avocado, cut into ¾-inch cubes
tortilla chips

Heat olive oil in a large stockpot over medium heat. Add onion, garlic, cilantro, cumin, jalapeno and scallions. Cook for 2 - 3 minutes. Add chicken broth and bring to a boil.

Simmer covered for 20 minutes. Just before serving add the diced cooked chicken or turkey and corn and heat for a few minutes.

Serve in individual bowls and garnish with tomatoes, cheese, avocado and tortilla chips.

chicken noodle soup
serves 4

Chicken noodle soup is an old fashioned comfort food and there are certain times when I just have to have it and nothing else will do. I tried repeatedly to make a great, flavorful, clear chicken broth that doesn't take a lot of time or effort. Then I discovered Swanson® Chicken Broth. It is so good and it tastes just like home-made, it's not worth the effort for me to make it from scratch. This is a great way to use up the leftover meat from a roasted chicken (page 45).

1 tablespoon olive oil
½ cup sliced baby carrots
½ cup diced celery
1 shallot, diced
2 tablespoons chopped fresh parsley
4 cups chicken broth
1 cup cooked diced chicken
1 cup of cooked spaghetti

Before cooking the spaghetti break it into 1-inch pieces. It's much easier to eat!

Heat the olive oil in a stockpot over medium heat. Add the carrots, celery and shallots and cook for about 5 minutes until tender. Do not let them brown. Add the chicken broth. Add the sautéed vegetables, parsley, cooked chicken and cooked spaghetti to the chicken broth. Heat on high until it simmers. Serve piping hot!

gazpacho
serves 6

Gazpacho is a very refreshing option to a large meal.

1 cup tomatoes, chopped, peeled and seeded
½ cup chopped celery
½ cup chopped seeded cucumber
½ cup chopped green pepper
½ cup chopped shallot
1 can (46 ounces) vegetable or tomato juice *(I prefer V-8®)*
1 tablespoon olive oil
Worcestershire to taste
Tabasco to taste
sour cream

Combine all ingredients in a large bowl. Refrigerate several hours before serving. Adjust seasoning to taste. Serve cold in soup bowls, mugs or margarita glasses. Top with a dollop of sour cream, and a sprig of parsley, fresh dill or a thin cucumber slice.

Increase or decrease the amount of vegetables depending on the amount you prefer.

billy's chili
serves 6

Before I met my husband Bill I had never tasted chili. I don't like beans and I thought all chili was chock full of beans. Bill's chili does not call for beans but you can certainly add them. The first couple of times he made chili for me it was too spicy. If you follow this recipe as written you'll find it may have a little kick; if it's too much just leave out the cayenne pepper. This is a true winner. All of our friends rave about this chili. For our annual Black and Blue Bowl Party (flag football game the Saturday before Thanksgiving) Bill makes the equivalent of 10 batches of chili. We serve it after the game along with a hot sauce bar (Bill has about 15 different hot sauces) and it's usually gone within the hour.

3 tablespoons vegetable oil
3 onions, chopped
3½ pounds of ground beef
6 tablespoons chili powder
2 cans (28 ounces each) tomato sauce
1 can (6 ounces) tomato paste
1 can (12 ounces) beer
¼ teaspoon basil
2 bay leaves
2 teaspoons fresh ground black pepper
cayenne pepper to taste
1½ tablespoons cilantro
2 tablespoons cumin powder

¾ teaspoon garlic powder
1½ teaspoons Italian seasoning
1 teaspoon paprika
1 tablespoon parsley
crushed red pepper taste
1 tablespoon sugar
¼ teaspoon tarragon
3 tablespoons Worcestershire sauce
½ cup cider vinegar
Tabasco
shredded cheddar cheese
chopped onions
diced jalapeno peppers

Heat oil in a stockpot over medium high heat. Sauté onions until tender; approximately 3 - 4 minutes. Add ground beef and brown. While the meat is browning add the chili powder. Once the meat has browned add the tomato sauce, tomato paste and beer and mix together thoroughly. Stir in the rest of the ingredients, except the cheese, onions and jalapeno peppers (they're for the garnish).

Bring to a boil then reduce heat and simmer for 3 hours. If chili becomes too thick, add water or beer to thin it out. Serve in individual chili bowls and top with cheddar cheese, chopped onions, jalapeno peppers and sour cream. To spice it up a bit add Tabasco and your favorite hot sauces. Bill especially likes Dave's Insanity Sauce. The flavor is enhanced if it's refrigerated overnight before serving, then reheated.

alternative serving suggestions

Serve over cooked pasta shells. The chili seeps into the shells. It's really good. Our friend Carter likes to add some cooked corn to his.

a note from bill

For years people have raved about my chili. I have never given this recipe out to anyone. The fact that I turned Niecie into a chili lover is testimony to this recipe. It alone is worth the cost of *the tiny kitchen*!

jambalaya

serves 4

⅓ cup butter
½ cup chopped scallions
½ cup chopped onions
1 large green pepper, seeded and diced
1 cup chopped celery
1 clove garlic
1 pound andouille sausage cut into bite-sized pieces
1 pound cooked shrimp, peeled and deveined
1 can (14.5 ounces) whole tomatoes
1 cup chicken broth
1 bay leaf
¼ teaspoon thyme
salt and cayenne pepper to taste
Tabasco to taste
1 cup uncooked white rice

Melt the butter over medium heat in a stockpot. Sauté scallions, onions, green pepper, celery and garlic until tender, about 5 minutes. Add the sausage and cook for 5 minutes. Add shrimp, tomatoes, chicken broth, bay leaf, thyme, salt, cayenne pepper and Tabasco. Stir in white rice. Simmer covered for 25 minutes until rice is tender. Add more chicken broth if jambalaya becomes too dry.

scotch broth

serves 6

This is a great way to use leftover leg of lamb (page 63) that still has some meat left on the bone. The barley cooked right in the liquid thickens the soup nicely. I remember the first time my mother made this was a snow day (yeah! no school!) and we'd all been playing out in the snow and cold. We'd pop into the house from time to time to get warm and the house smelled so good. We kept sneaking tastes of the scotch broth and by the time we were ready to eat there wasn't much left.

    1 leftover leg of lamb, meat still on the bone (page 63)
    8 cups chicken or beef broth
    ½ cup uncooked barley
    1 cup diced carrots
    1 cup diced celery
    1 small white turnip, peeled and diced
    1 shallot, diced
    salt and pepper to taste
    3 tablespoons chopped parsley

Place the leg of lamb in a large stockpot and add the chicken or beef broth. Add the barley and bring to a boil. Simmer partially covered for 1 hour. Add the carrots, celery, turnip, shallot, salt and pepper. Add more broth or water if necessary. Simmer for 30 minutes. Remove the meat from the bones and discard the bone. Just before serving stir in parsley.

beef burgundy

serves 6

4 tablespoons olive oil
½ cup flour
2 teaspoons salt
1 teaspoon pepper
1 teaspoon celery seed
1 teaspoon dried thyme
½ teaspoon marjoram
2 ½ pounds lean beef stew meat
    cut into 1-inch cubes

3 cups beef broth
1 cup dry red wine
1 bay leaf
1 tablespoon Dijon mustard
12 baby carrots
12 small white boiling onions,
    trimmed and peeled
2 large potatoes, peeled and cut into
    1-inch cubes

Heat the olive oil over medium heat in a large stockpot. Mix the flour, salt, pepper, celery seed, thyme and marjoram together in a bowl. Roll the beef cubes in the flour mixture to fully coat the cubes. If there is leftover flour mixture, set aside. Brown the meat a few pieces at a time and set aside.

After browning all the meat add the beef broth, wine, bay leaf and mustard. Return the meat to the pot and cover and simmer for 1½ hours. Add the carrots, onions and potatoes. Cook for 30 more minutes. The stew is done when the potatoes, carrots and onions are fork tender. Remove the meat, potatoes and vegetables from the pot and cover to keep warm. If there is remaining flour mixture, place it in a small bowl and add 1 - 2 tablespoons of the hot liquid (adding the flour mixture dry directly into the large pot of hot liquid will create lumps in the liquid) and mix until smooth. Then stir this mixture into the pot of liquid. Bring the liquid to a boil to thicken to the consistency you like. Serve in soup bowls with warm crusty bread.

pasta bolognese

serves 6

2 pounds ground beef
2 pounds ground veal
2 tablespoons olive oil
1 onion, diced
1 clove garlic, minced
1 stalk celery, finely diced
2 cans (29 ounces each) tomato sauce
2 tablespoons basil
3 tablespoons oregano

2 teaspoons salt
1 teaspoon pepper
1 bay leaf
1 cup dry red wine
2 cans (6 ounces each) tomato
   paste
1/8 teaspoon cinnamon
4 cups cooked spaghetti
Parmesan cheese

In a large stockpot brown the beef and veal over medium heat. Remove the meat and set aside. Drain the liquid from the pot. In the same pot heat the olive oil over medium heat. Add the onion, garlic and celery and cook for 5 minutes. Stir in the meat, tomato sauce, basil, oregano, salt, pepper and bay leaf. Simmer covered for 45 minutes. In a small bowl mix the tomato paste, red wine and cinnamon until thoroughly blended, and then stir into the meat sauce. Simmer covered for 15 minutes. Remove the bay leaf. Serve over the cooked spaghetti and sprinkle with Parmesan cheese.

pesto penne
serves 4

1 tablespoon olive oil
1 clove garlic, minced
¼ pound Prosciutto, cut into bite-sized pieces
2 roma tomatoes, seeded and diced or 12 cherry or grape tomatoes, cut
   in half
1 container (7 ounces) pesto sauce
2 cups cooked penne
½ cup shredded mozzarella

In a medium saucepan heat the olive oil over medium heat. Add the garlic and cook for 1 minute. Add the Prosciutto and tomatoes and cook for 2 minutes. Add the pesto and heat for 1 - 2 minutes. Add the cooked penne and mozzarella and toss to coat thoroughly. Serve in pasta bowls.

asparagus risotto
serves 4

Creamy risotto is a wonderfully rich and filling dish. A small portion served with a crisp green salad makes a great meal. Arborio is actually an Italian rice that has an outer layer of starch. During the cooking process of constant stirring while gradually adding hot liquid the starch dissolves to give it the rich creamy texture while the rice remains chewy.

2 tablespoon olive oil
2 tablespoons butter
1 shallot, diced
1 clove garlic, diced
2 cups arborio rice
salt and pepper to taste
1 teaspoon lemon zest
½ cup dry white wine
4 cups chicken broth brought to a boil
½ cup grated Parmesan cheese
1 cup steamed asparagus (cut into 1-inch pieces)

Melt the olive oil and butter in a large saucepan over medium heat. Sauté the shallot and garlic for 2 - 3 minutes. Add the rice and salt and pepper and cook for 5 minutes, stirring constantly until it's a golden brown. Add the lemon zest and wine and cook until the wine is absorbed. Stirring constantly, gradually add the boiling chicken broth. Cover and cook for 15 minutes or until the liquid is absorbed and the rice is creamy. Remove from heat and stir in the Parmesan cheese and asparagus. Let stand for 2 - 3 minutes before serving.

potatoes, grains & veggies

sea salt roasted potatoes - 84

dilled new potatoes - 84

spiced creamy potatoes - 85

lumpy red mashed potatoes - 86

old fashioned mashed potatoes - 86

grains - 87

broiled tomatoes - 89

vegetables hollandaise - 90

grandma sullivan's rutabaga - 91

harvard beets - 92

gingered carrots - 93

Potatoes are wonderfully versatile in terms of preparation methods and resulting textures and tastes. They take on a very creamy texture by mashing, crisp by roasting and very tender by boiling.

I've come to appreciate the wide variety of rice and grains available. I've included those I most frequently prepare—wild, brown, basmati and long grain white rice as well as couscous. Couscous is so light and soft I just love it. It only takes a couple of minutes to prepare and is tasty whether it's served hot or cold. I often add it cold on top of a green salad with sliced chicken and vinaigrette dressing. Cooking it in the chicken broth gives it plenty of flavor on its own. There are endless varieties of grains I have tried such as barley, millet, wheat berry, oats and kasha but I typically make it once then end up throwing away the unused, uncooked leftovers about six months later. I just stick with the basics I know I'll use.

I like to keep vegetables fresh and uncomplicated, preferably steaming them to bring them to the peak of their flavor. The desired goal is a colorful, healthy accompaniment splendidly presented with an entrée.

sea salt roasted potatoes
serves 4

These potatoes are great. The two tablespoons of sea salt sounds like a lot, but it gives them a delicious flavor. They're crispy on the outside and very soft on the inside. Serve them with roasted chicken, beef tenderloin or pork tenderloin.

3 pounds new red potatoes
½ cup of Newman's Own® Olive
    Oil and Vinegar Dressing
2 tablespoons sea salt
fresh ground black pepper to
    taste

Preheat the oven to 400°.

Wash and cut the potatoes (leaving the skin on) in half or quarters depending on the size to make bite sized pieces. Boil the potatoes in salted water for approximately 8 minutes. Drain the potatoes and let cool for a few minutes. Pour ¼ cup dressing in the bottom of a roasting pan, and coat the pan. Sprinkle 1 tablespoon of sea salt and pepper to taste on top. Place the potatoes, skin side up, and brush the remaining ¼ cup dressing on top of the potatoes to coat. Sprinkle remaining 1 tablespoon of sea salt and pepper to taste over the potatoes. Bake for 30 minutes.

alternative

Put the dressing, salt and pepper in a large plastic bag. Put the raw cut potatoes in the bag. Tie the bag to close and shake vigorously to coat. Put the coated potatoes into the roasting pan and bake at 400° for about an hour.

dilled new potatoes

After boiling the potatoes drain them. Return to the pot and toss with 2 tablespoons butter and 2 tablespoons dill.

spiced creamy potatoes
serves 8

The creamy texture of these potatoes will send your guests back for seconds. I make several batches of these for Easter Afternoon Supper at my parents' with all our relatives. They all love spicy food so I make all except one batch with cayenne pepper. Every year we run out, no matter how many batches I make.

> 5 pounds white potatoes, peeled and cut in half
> salt and pepper to taste
> pinch of nutmeg
> cayenne pepper to taste
> 1 cup cheddar cheese, shredded
> 4 tablespoons butter
> 2 cups half and half
> 2 tablespoons Parmesan cheese

Boil the potatoes in salted water until fork tender (about 15 minutes). Drain and let cool for 20 minutes. Once cooled, grate the potatoes.

Preheat the oven to 350°. Lightly grease a deep baking dish or a pie plate. Place a layer of grated potatoes (enough to cover the bottom). Sprinkle the top with salt, pepper, nutmeg and cayenne pepper. Add a layer of cheddar cheese on top. Alternate layers of potatoes, salt, pepper, nutmeg, cayenne pepper and cheddar cheese. End with a layer of potatoes. I usually end up with three layers of potatoes and two layers of cheese. Melt the butter and whisk into the half and half. Pour over the potatoes, sprinkle the top with Parmesan cheese. Bake for 30 minutes.

mashed potatoes

lumpy red
serves 4

3 pounds new red potatoes
½ cup butter
¾ cup heavy cream

½ cup sour cream
1 tablespoon tarragon
2 tablespoons Parmesan cheese

Preheat the oven to 350°.

Wash the potatoes and cut in half (leaving the skin on). Boil the potatoes in salted water for approximately 8 -10 minutes until fork tender. While potatoes are cooking melt the butter with the heavy cream over low heat. Stir in sour cream until smooth. Drain the potatoes. Using a potato masher, mash the potatoes with the butter, heavy cream, sour cream and tarragon. Leave the mixture lumpy. Spoon the mixture into a lightly greased baking dish. Sprinkle with Parmesan cheese and bake for 30 minutes.

old fashioned
serves 6

3 pounds white potatoes
4 tablespoons butter

1 cup heavy cream
salt and pepper to taste

Wash and cut the potatoes in quarters. Boil the potatoes in salted water for approximately 15 minutes until fork tender. While potatoes are cooking melt the butter with the heavy cream over low heat. Drain the potatoes. Using a potato masher, mash the potatoes with the butter, heavy cream and salt and pepper until smooth.

grains

Here are basic cooking techniques for several types of rice. Wild rice (which is actually the seed of an aquatic grass) pops open when it's cooked and has a rich brown color and nutty taste and texture. Similarly, brown rice has a nutty taste with a chewy texture. Basmati rice is highly aromatic with a light, sweet taste.

wild rice
serves 6

> 1 box (4 ounces) wild rice
> 2¾ cups chicken broth
> ½ cup diced celery

Combine rice, chicken broth and celery in a saucepan. Bring to a boil. Reduce heat and simmer covered for 1 hour. Let rice cool.

brown rice
serves 4

> 1 cup brown rice
> 2 cups beef broth
> 1 teaspoon butter

Combine rice, beef broth and butter in a saucepan. Bring to a boil. Reduce heat and simmer covered for 45 minutes. Let rice cool.

---

couscous
serves 4

1 cup of couscous
1 cup of chicken broth

Bring chicken broth to a boil in a small saucepan. Stir in the couscous. Cover and remove from heat. Let stand for 5 minutes. Fluff with a fork. Makes 4 cups.

basmati rice
serves 4

1 cup basmati rice
2¼ cups water

Bring the water to a boil in a saucepan. Stir in the rice. Reduce heat and simmer covered for 20 minutes until all the liquid has been absorbed.

long grain white rice
serves 4

1 cup long grain white rice
2¼ cups water
½ teaspoon salt
1 teaspoon butter

Bring the water to a boil in a saucepan. Add salt and butter. Stir in the rice. Reduce heat and simmer covered for 20 minutes until all the liquid has been absorbed.

spanish rice
serves 4

1 cup long grain rice
2 tablespoons vegetable oil
¼ cup chopped onion
1 jalapeno pepper, seeded and diced
4 ounces tomato sauce
2 cups water
½ teaspoon garlic powder
½ teaspoon salt
½ teaspoon pepper

Heat the oil in a saucepan over medium heat. Add the rice and cook until brown, about 5 minutes. Add the onion and jalapeno and sauté for 2 minutes. Add the tomato sauce, water and spices. Bring to a boil. Cover and simmer for 15 minutes until all the liquid is absorbed.

For added flavor for rices or couscous add 2 tablespoons of parsley, chives, dill or any other spice of choice. Mix the spices with the dry rice or couscous before adding it to the liquid.

broiled tomatoes

serves 4

2 medium sized tomatoes
2 tablespoons Parmesan cheese
Newman's Own® Balsamic Vinaigrette

Preheat the broiler.

Remove the core from the tomatoes and cut in half. Brush the cut sides with vinaigrette. Place the tomatoes, cut side up, on a baking sheet and sprinkle the tops with Parmesan cheese. Broil for 10 minutes.

vegetables hollandaise

serves 6

1 bunch asparagus
2 crowns broccoli
1 cup baby carrots
1 package McCormick®
    Hollandaise Sauce Mix

Wash and trim the asparagus. Asparagus breaks at a natural breaking point where the stalk is too tough to eat by bending the non-leafy end until it breaks off. Trim the broccoli and cut into bite sized pieces. Steam the vegetables together until tender (about 8 minutes) in a stockpot fitted with a steamer. Add the carrots and broccoli first and let them steam for a few minutes before adding the asparagus.

Prepare the hollandaise sauce mix according to the directions on the package. Serve over the hot steamed vegetables.

steamed vegetables

I steam almost all my fresh vegetables: green beans, peas, spinach, corn, carrots, broccoli, snow peas and cauliflower. For a nice touch toss steamed vegetables with butter and slivered almonds.

A steamer can be purchased for a couple of dollars and expands and contracts to fit a variety of pot sizes. To steam, fit a pot with the steamer, and then fill the pot with water to just below the base of the steamer. Bring the water to a boil then add the vegetables. Cover the pot with a tight fitting lid. Turn the heat to low. I like my vegetables a bit crunchy so I find 8 minutes the perfect cooking time. Adjust the cooking time depending on your desired tenderness.

grandma sullivan's rutabaga (yellow turnip)

serves 4 - 6

This is a *must* with roasted turkey (page 50) and roasted leg of lamb (page 63) in the Sullivan household. All guests must try it. After several visits they're hooked.

1 large rutabaga or several small ones
4 tablespoons butter
⅓ - ½ cup brown sugar

Cut the rutabaga into cubes with serrated bread knife on a cutting board. You'll have to use some elbow grease—it's tough! Then slice the skin off the pieces. Cook covered in salted boiling water to cover until tender for approximately 20 - 30 minutes. Drain and place back on heat for a minute to dry out. Mash with a potato masher leaving some lumps. Add butter and brown sugar to taste. Serve immediately or make a day ahead and heat in frying pan with butter.

harvard beets
serves 4

This is another *must have* with roasted leg of lamb (page 63).

    1 can (15 ounces) whole, sliced or diced cooked beets
    ½ cup sugar
    2 teaspoons cornstarch
    ¼ cup cider vinegar
    ¼ cup water
    2 tablespoons butter

Mix sugar and cornstarch in a small saucepan. Add vinegar and water and stir to remove any lumps. Bring to a boil and boil gently while stirring until thickened about 5 minutes. Add the beets and remove from heat for 30 minutes or until ready to serve. Reheat and add butter.

gingered carrots

serves 2

1 cup baby carrots
1 tablespoon butter
¼ teaspoon ginger
1 teaspoon brown sugar

Steam the carrots until fork tender, about 8 minutes. Remove the carrots from the steamer. Empty the water from the pot and return the carrots to the pot. Toss with the butter, ginger and brown sugar and cook over low heat for 1 - 2 minutes.

desserts

toffee bars - 96

light nut bars - 97

grandma dexter's butter cookies - 98

grandma dexter's pound cake - 99

decadent chocolate cake - 100

pumpkin chiffon pie - 102

pumpkin mousse with ginger man cookies - 103

apple pie with hard sauce - 104

mince pie - 105

chocolate mousse - 106

meringue pie crust - 107

coconut pie crust - 107

individual meringue nests - 108

overnight meringues - 108

chocolate roll - 109

mocha brownies - 111

poached pears with raspberry coulis - 112

melon with lime sorbet - 113

don't think that just because you have a tiny kitchen that you have to either rely on store bought desserts or cookie and cake mixes. I have brought together here some of my favorite desserts that are a little bit different, go a long way and are impressive. They are easy to make and many can be made days ahead of time.

I was having a big Christmas party one year and remember making Grandma Dexter's Pound Cake sitting in my living room one evening while watching TV. I only had a hand eggbeater but beating in each of the five eggs by hand wasn't that monotonous with the TV to distract me. It probably took about 15 minutes of beating, but it was worth it! My grandmother would tell me of the days when she didn't have even a hand eggbeater and had to do all the beating by hand with a wooden spoon.

My Grandmother Dexter was a wonderful baker. She baked almost every day. I have several of her recipes here as they are still used frequently today by my family.

I offer a couple of different pie crusts and fillings in this chapter that are very versatile. Be creative as to how you use them. Mix and match the fillings and crusts. Try the pumpkin chiffon filling in the coconut crust — it's delicious!

If you're a chocolate chip cookie fan, you'll have to try the toffee bars. I love the rich buttery taste of them. My mother used to make them every day in the summer. They're easy to make and a huge hit. I only make them for parties now because they are so addictive.

toffee bars

makes 4 dozen

1 cup butter, softened
1 cup brown sugar
1 teaspoon vanilla
2 cups flour
1 bag (12 ounces) chocolate chips
1 cup chopped walnuts

Preheat the oven to 325°.

Cream together butter, brown sugar and vanilla. Stir in flour and mix well. Add chocolate chips and walnuts and stir until well mixed. The dough is rather stiff at this point. Spread the dough into an ungreased jelly roll pan. (Here's a hint: divide the dough into six pieces and distribute evenly in the jelly roll pan. It's a lot easier to spread six small pieces than it is to spread one big piece). Place a piece of wax paper or plastic wrap over the dough. Use a rolling pin or your hands to flatten the dough. Make sure the dough is spread evenly throughout the pan. Bake for 25 minutes. Cut into 1 x 1½-inch bars immediately after taking them out of the oven. Leave in the pan until completely cooled.

hint

Make sure you cut the cookies immediately after taking them out of the oven; if you let them cool they will be too hard to cut.

Years ago I brought a batch of these to the office and my boss loved them so he asked me for the recipe. One Saturday night I was home watching TV when my boss called. He had made the toffee bars but said they didn't come out right and swore I had left something out of the recipe on purpose. I asked him what was wrong with them and he said they were too hard to cut and they were crumbling. He forgot to cut them when they were hot! I laughed hysterically because he had a pan full of crumbs from trying to cut them once they cooled.

light nut bars

makes 3 dozen

This is a great recipe as it takes no more than 5 minutes to prepare and get in the oven.

4 eggs
2 cups brown sugar
1⅓ cups sifted flour
1 teaspoon baking soda
½ teaspoon salt
2 cups chopped pecans or walnuts
½ cup powdered sugar

variations

For a dipping biscotti-like dessert, cut into bars 1 x 4-inch and let stand uncovered overnight to dry out.

For a more cake-like dessert, bake in a 9 x 13-inch glass baking dish and bake for about 20 - 25 minutes. Cut into 3 inch squares and serve with whipped cream flavored with cinnamon.

Preheat the oven to 350°.

Beat eggs and brown sugar together until light and fluffy. Fold in flour, baking soda and salt. Stir in the nuts and spread into a greased jelly roll pan. Bake for 20 - 25 minutes until a toothpick comes out dry. Cut into bars (about 1 x 1½-inches) while hot. Put powdered sugar in a large baggie. Put several squares in the baggie and shake until fully coated. Remove and cool on a rack. Continue until all bars are coated.

grandma dexter's butter cookies
makes 3 dozen

2 sticks butter, softened
⅔ cup powdered sugar
1 teaspoon vanilla
2 cups flour
½ cup raspberry jam

Cream together the butter, sugar and vanilla until well mixed. Add the flour and stir until well mixed. Refrigerate the dough for about 1 hour. Preheat the oven to 325°. Roll the dough into 1-inch balls and place on an ungreased cookie sheet. Press the center of each ball down with your thumb to create a well. Place a dab of raspberry jam in the center of each cookie. Bake for 8 minutes. Remove and cool on a cake rack.

---

variations

In addition to the raspberry jam filling, Grandma Dexter used to fill the centers with a couple of chocolate chips, nuts or candied cherries and other fruits. She would also make the cookies crescent shaped and dip the ends in melted chocolate, then coconut. Yum!

My favorite variation of this recipe is by adding ½ cup chopped walnuts or pecans to the dough; baking the cookies in the ball shape then rolling in powdered sugar while still warm.

---

grandma dexter's pound cake
serves 15

This is a classic. The recipe doubles well to make two cakes at once which is a great timesaver if you're having a crowd. The cake's flavor improves after a day or two. Make ahead and keep covered with plastic wrap. It also freezes very well.

1 cup butter (softened)
1²⁄₃ cups sugar
5 eggs
2 cups *cake* flour
¼ teaspoon salt

Preheat the oven to 300°.

    Cream butter and sugar until light and fluffy. Beat in eggs, one at a time until creamy. Fold in the flour and salt and pour into greased and floured 10-inch tube pan. Bake for 1 - 1½ hours until a toothpick comes out dry. Let cool for 10 - 15 minutes. Remove from the pan by running a knife around the edges of the pan. If it seems to stick to the bottom, tap the bottom of the pan to loosen. Turn upside down on a cake rack, then transfer to plate right side up then slide back onto the cake rack to cool. Just before serving sprinkle with powdered sugar. Cut into ½-inch slices to serve.

---

variation

Invert the cake upside down so the bottom becomes the top. Drizzle with lemon or orange glaze and let it drip down the sides.

For the glaze:
¼ cup lemon or orange juice
¼ cup powdered sugar
Stir enough powdered sugar into the orange juice or lemon juice until it can be easily drizzled over the cake.

---

decadent chocolate cake
serves 12

1 cup boiling water
3 ounces unsweetened chocolate
8 tablespoons butter
1 teaspoon vanilla extract
2 cups granulated sugar
2 eggs, separated
1 teaspoon baking soda
½ cup sour cream
2 cups less 2 tablespoons flour, sifted
1 teaspoon baking powder
Chocolate Frosting Recipe (recipe follows)

Preheat the oven to 350°.

Grease and flour a 10-inch tube pan. Knock out excess. In a large bowl pour boiling water over the chocolate and butter and let stand until melted. Stir in vanilla and sugar then whisk in egg yolks, one at a time, blending well after each addition.

Mix baking soda and sour cream and whisk into chocolate mixture.

Sift flour and baking powder together and add to the batter, mixing thoroughly. Beat egg whites until stiff but not dry. Stir a quarter of the egg whites thoroughly into the batter. Scoop remaining egg whites on top of the batter and gently fold together. Pour batter into the prepared pan. Set on the middle rack of the oven and bake for 40 - 50 minutes, or until the edges have pulled away from the sides of the pan and a cake tester inserted into the center comes out clean.

Cool in pan for 10 minutes; unmold and cool completely before frosting.

chocolate frosting

>   2 tablespoons butter
>   ¾ cup semisweet chocolate chips
>   6 tablespoons heavy cream
>   1¼ cups sifted powdered sugar
>   1 teaspoon vanilla extract

Place all ingredients in a heavy saucepan over low heat and whisk until smooth. Cool slightly; add more sugar if necessary to achieve a spreading consistency. Spread on cake while frosting is still warm.

Excerpted form The Silver Palate Cookbook
Copyright © 1982 by Sheila Lukins & Julee Rosso
Used by permission of Workman Publishing Co., Inc., New York
All Rights Reserved

author's note

This is by far the best chocolate cake recipe I have ever come across. It is a standard at any large party we have and guests always ask for the recipe. It's a favorite of my niece, Katie, and nephew, Matthew.

The frosting is so good that I double the recipe for one cake. This cake freezes very well and can be frozen unfrosted for several days before using. In fact it's easier to frost the cake while it is frozen, so make it a few days before you are planning to use it, and freeze it. The day you use the cake, make the frosting; remove cake from the freezer and frost while the icing is still warm.

The cake is also nice without the frosting, dusted with powdered sugar and served sliced with whipped cream. This recipe doubles very easily for 2 cakes.

pumpkin chiffon pie
serves 8 to 10

I am not a pumpkin pie fan, but this recipe, which my mother has always made, is to die for. Each Thanksgiving my parents host an open house in the evening right about the time you're craving a turkey sandwich and a piece of pumpkin pie. Some people come just for this pumpkin pie. Last year my husband's company was having a Christmas party and dessert contest at work so he asked me to make this pie because he wanted to be guaranteed to win. I made it and he won first place —$100. Don't even think of making this with a pre-made graham cracker crust. It won't do it justice!

This filling makes enough so you can stretch it into two pies.

graham cracker crust

This is a fantastic crust. It only takes a few minutes to make and is a thousand times better than any store bought graham cracker crust.

> 2 cups graham cracker crumbs
> ⅓ cup sugar
> ⅔ cup melted butter

Preheat the oven to 375°.

Combine sugar and graham cracker crumbs until well mixed. Stir in the melted butter and mix thoroughly. Spread into a greased 9-inch pie plate patting it down on the bottom and sides. Bake for 8 minutes. Remove and cool before filling.

for the filling

¾ cup brown sugar

1 envelope unflavored gelatin

½ teaspoon salt

1 teaspoon cinnamon

¼ teaspoon ginger

3 eggs, separated

¾ cup milk

1¼ cups canned pumpkin (*not* pumpkin pie mix)

⅓ cup sugar

1 pint whipping cream

2 tablespoons powdered sugar

nutmeg

---

pumpkin mousse with ginger man cookies

Make the pumpkin chiffon pie filing recipe. Spoon the pumpkin mixture into individual ramekins, demitasse cups, punch cups or any other individual serving cups. Refrigerate for 1 hour. When ready to serve top with whipped cream and serve with Pepperidge Farm® Ginger Man Homestyle Cookies.

Combine brown sugar, gelatin, salt and spices in a pot. Lightly beat the egg yolks. Combine egg yolks and milk in a bowl and stir until mixed thoroughly. Stir the egg yolk and milk mixture into the brown sugar mixture and cook the mixture over medium heat until it boils, stirring constantly. Remove from the heat and stir in the pumpkin. Put in the refrigerator to cool approximately 20 minutes while you're beating the egg whites. Beat egg whites until stiff gradually adding the sugar. Test the pumpkin mixture by dropping a spoonful. If it holds its shape, it's ready. Stir in a couple of tablespoons of the beaten egg white. Then fold in the remaining egg white. Pour into graham cracker crust and refrigerate for 2 hours. When ready to serve whip the cream with the powdered sugar and spread over the pie. Sprinkle with nutmeg and serve.

apple pie with hard sauce
serves 8 - 10

4 - 5 granny smith apples
½ cup sugar
⅛ teaspoon ground cloves
¼ teaspoon cinnamon
1 teaspoon nutmeg
1 teaspoon lemon juice
2 tablespoons butter cut into pieces
1 tablespoon flour
1 package unbaked pie crust*
1 egg, mixed lightly with 1 tablespoon
   cream

hard sauce
serves 8 - 10

2 sticks butter, softened
1 cup powdered sugar
2 teaspoons brandy or cognac

Whip butter and gradually add sugar beating until creamy. Add brandy or cognac while beating. May be refrigerated for up to a week. Serve at room temperature.

Preheat the oven to 425°.

   Place one unbaked pie crust in bottom and up the sides of an ungreased 9-inch pie plate. In a medium bowl slice apples and add the sugar, ground cloves, cinnamon, nutmeg and lemon juice. Mix lightly and pour into the unbaked pie crust. Dot with the butter pieces then sprinkle with flour. Top with the second crust and seal the crusts together with cold water. Crimp the edges of pie crust with a fork and cut off any excess crust. Prick the top crust with a fork in 6 places to release steam. Brush the top of the pie with the egg wash. Cover edges of pie crust with strips of foil to prevent them from burning. Bake for 25 - 30 minutes until the crust is a nice golden brown. Just before serving dust with powdered sugar and serve with hard sauce. * *I prefer the Pillsbury® brand.*

mince pie
serves 8 - 10

This is a three-minute recipe and can't be beat. My mother makes this pie twice a year: once at Thanksgiving and once for their friend Ernie's birthday. Ernie and my dad were classmates together at West Point and Ernie and his wife Caroline have been coming to my parent's Thanksgiving evening get-together for at least the last twenty years. Ernie comes specifically for this mince pie. Since he loves it so, my mother started a tradition of making it for him for his birthday.

> 1 package unbaked refrigerated pie crust*
> 1 jar (20.5 ounces) Crosse and Blackwell® Mince Meat with Rum and
>   Brandy (no other brand can compare)
> 1 egg, mixed lightly with 1 tablespoons cream

Preheat the oven to 425°.

   Place unbaked pie crust in bottom and up sides of an ungreased 9-inch pie plate. Fill with the mince meat. Top with the second crust and seal the crusts together with cold water. Crimp the edges of pie crust with a fork. Cut off any excess crust. Prick the top crust with a fork in 6 places to release steam. Brush the top of the pie with the egg wash. Cover edges of pie crust with strips of foil to prevent them from burning. Bake for 25 - 30 minutes until the crust is a nice golden brown. Just before serving dust with powdered sugar and serve with hard sauce and/or whipped cream. * *I prefer the Pillsbury® brand.*

chocolate mousse
serves 8 - 10

4 ounces sweet chocolate
2 tablespoons strong black coffee or Grand Marnier
1 teaspoon vanilla
1 cup heavy cream

Combine chocolate with coffee or Grand Marnier in a sauce pan over low heat. Stir until the mixture is smooth and chocolate is melted. Cool 10 - 15 minutes. Stir in vanilla. Whip the heavy cream. Fold the melted chocolate into the whipped cream. Refrigerate for 2 hours. Serve in champagne glasses, demitasse cups or other small individual serving cups. This is very rich so a little goes a long way. Serve with overnight meringues (page 108) on the side. Top with fresh raspberries.

---

variation

This is also an excellent pie filling. Fill the meringue crust or the coconut crust (next page) with the chocolate mousse. Refrigerate for 2 hours before serving. Just before serving top with whipped cream and garnish with chocolate curls or dust with cocoa.

---

meringue pie crust
makes 1 crust

I can't tell you how easy this is to make, how impressive it looks, how good it tastes and how light it is. You'll have to try it for yourself! But, don't try making meringues on a rainy day if you don't have air conditioning. The humidity will prevent them from drying out completely and they will be sticky.

4 egg whites
¼ teaspoon of cream of tartar
1 cup sugar

Preheat the oven to 275°.

Beat the egg whites with the cream of tartar adding the sugar slowly. Beat until shiny peaks form when the beater is lifted. Grease a 9-inch pie plate very well, including the sides but not the top edge.

Spread mixture into the pie plate, making sure to not have it too thick on the bottom; but making it nice and fluffy on the sides. Bake for 1 hour. Cool away from drafty areas.

coconut pie crust

2 cups shredded coconut
½ cup melted butter

Preheat the oven to 325°.
Mix the coconut and melted butter together. Press into a 9-inch greased pie plate. Bake 8 minutes. Remove and cool before filling.

filling suggestions

Whipped cream topped with berries, chocolate mousse (page 106), pumpkin mousse (page 103), or fresh fruit with raspberry coulis (page 112).

individual meringue nests
makes 8 nests

This is a great way to let everyone create their own desert. Have an assortment of fillings and fruits and let each guest create his own treat.

Prepare the recipe for the meringue pie crust. Preheat the oven to 275°. Line a jelly roll pan with wax paper. For each nest, drop ½ cup of beaten egg white onto the wax paper and with the back of a spoon gently form a hollow to create a nest. Leave about 1 inch between each nest. Bake for 1 hour.

filling suggestions

Sorbet, ice cream, whipped cream topped with berries, chocolate mousse (page 106), pumpkin mousse (page 103), fresh fruit with raspberry coulis (page 112).

---

overnight meringues
makes 3 dozen

Make these at night before you go to bed and in the morning you have a wonderful treat.

Preheat the oven to 350°.

Prepare the meringue pie crust recipe (page 107) but cut all the ingredients in half (unless you want to make 6 dozen cookies). Fold 1 cup of chopped walnuts into beaten egg whites. Line a jelly roll pan with wax paper. Drop the egg whites by the teaspoonful onto the wax paper. You do not need to leave room in between as they will not spread. Place in the oven and immediately turn off the oven and leave in overnight. Do not open the oven, no matter how curious you are. In the morning remove from the oven and remove from the wax paper. Store in an airtight container until ready to serve.

---

chocolate roll

serves 8

This is such an elegant looking dessert and it is very light. My mother used to serve this at her dinner parties back in the 1960's and 1970's. We used to wait anxiously for her to cut off the crusty edges. My brother and sisters and I each got a strip. The morning after the party we'd eat the leftovers from the party, if there were any! Although the directions look cumbersome, they really are not. I remember my brother Robert made it once and didn't use the wax paper and waited too long to roll it. What a mess!

    5 eggs
    1 cup powdered sugar
    3 tablespoons unsweetened cocoa powder
    1 pint whipping cream
    3 - 4 tablespoons powdered sugar
    cocoa for dusting

Preheat the oven to 350°.

Separate the eggs and place the whites in a large bowl and the yolks in a medium bowl. Grease the bottom and sides of a jelly roll pan. Line the jelly roll pan with wax paper, including the sides and press securely so that it sticks to the pan. Butter the wax paper, including the sides.

In a small bowl mix the sugar and cocoa together. Beat the egg whites until soft peaks form. Add the sugar and cocoa a little at a time while continuing to beat until the mixture is stiff. In a separate bowl, and without washing the beater, beat the egg yolks until thick. Fold the egg yolks into the egg white/cocoa mixture. Spread evenly in the jelly roll pan. Bake for 20 minutes or until the cake shrinks from the sides of the pan.

While the cake is baking spread on the counter either a clean dish towel or paper towels large enough to fit the cake and dust with powdered sugar. Upon removing the cake from the oven turn onto the towel and remove the pan. Immediately remove the wax paper very gently, a little at a time, starting at one end and working your way to the other end. You may have to help it along with the edge of a knife inserted between the cake and the wax paper. If it really sticks place a clean damp towel on wax paper for 20 to 60 seconds. Cut the crispy edges off the cake (about ½-inch on each side). You can eat those edges now! Dust the cake with powdered sugar. This keeps the cake from sticking to the towel in the next step. Immediately roll up the cake (with the towel) and cool slightly, about 10 minutes.

Meanwhile, whip the cream with 3 tablespoons of powdered sugar until it is quite stiff (but don't turn it to butter!). Unroll the cake and spread with half the whipped cream leaving about ½-inch border. Depending on the length of the cake you want, gently roll up the cake either from the long end or the short end, using the towel to help you roll. Gently lift the cake onto your serving platter. Chill covered for 2 - 3 hours. Before serving spread the remaining whipped cream on the outside of the cake to completely cover it. This may be done an hour or so before serving. Immediately before serving sprinkle, with cocoa and garnish the platter with strawberries or raspberries. Cut with a sharp knife into one inch slices.

mocha brownies
makes 2 dozen

¾ cup flour

⅓ cup hot cocoa mix *(I prefer Ghiradelli® Chocolate Mocha)*

¼ teaspoon baking powder

¼ teaspoon salt

2 eggs

1 cup sugar

⅓ cup melted butter, preferably unsalted

1 teaspoon vanilla extract

¾ cup chopped walnuts

Preheat the oven to 350°.

   Stir flour, cocoa mix, baking powder and salt together in a small bowl. Beat eggs lightly in a medium bowl. Stir in sugar, melted butter and vanilla. Add the cocoa mixture and stir until just blended, then add the nuts. Pour into an 8 x 8-inch greased pan and bake for 25 - 30 minutes. Cool in pan and cut into squares.

---

variation

You may substitute Ghiradelli® Cocoa and Ground Chocolate or Ghiradelli's Chocolate Hazelnut Hot Chocolate Mix for the Chocolate Mocha.

---

poached pears with raspberry coulis
serves 4

4 ripe pears
1 cup dry white wine
½ cup of sugar
1½ cups of water
zest of 1 lemon
½ teaspoon of vanilla
½ cup of orange marmalade

raspberry coulis

½ cup currant jelly
1 jar good quality raspberry jam,
seedless if available
¼ - ½ cup orange juice
½ teaspoon lemon juice

Heat all ingredients together over low heat until melted. Serve warm.

Peel the pears leaving the stem intact. Cut out the core from the bottom. Cut off a piece from the bottom if necessary for them to stand up straight. Combine wine, sugar, 1½ cups of water, lemon zest and vanilla in a stock pot and bring to a boil. Add the pears and more water if necessary to cover the pears. Simmer gently 8 - 12 minutes until just tender. Remove the pears to a bowl. Bring the liquid to a full boil and reduce by at least one half. Stir in the marmalade. Reduce heat and stir until marmalade is blended in. Pour over the pears. Cool and chill in the refrigerator. May be served chilled or at room temperature. To serve place on dessert plate. Drizzle with the liquid and raspberry coulis.

melon with lime sorbet

serves 4

This makes a cool refreshing dessert on a hot summer day. The lime enhances the flavor of the melon.

     1 cantaloupe or honeydew melon
     the juice of 1 lime
     1 quart lime sorbet

Cut the melon into quarters and remove the seeds and skin. Season each quarter with the lime juice. Place a scoop of lime sorbet in the cavity of the melon and garnish with mint leaves or fresh berries.

---

variation

Orange or raspberry sorbet offer the same refreshing taste as the lime. You can also add 1 - 2 tablespoons of honey to the lime juice and stir together before seasoning the melon.

---

the tiny kitchen entertains

ntertaining! It's one of my favorite pastimes. I love gathering together with family and friends to celebrate a holiday, special occasion or just because. I welcome the opportunity to create pleasant memories through a warm and inviting atmosphere, sumptuous food and wonderful conversation. Entertaining can be as simple as a dinner for two for an intimate time or a large cocktail party to bring old and new friends together for an evening of mingling. Whatever the event, entertaining shouldn't be viewed as a project, nor should it be a source of stress. You should have fun and be energized from the beginning when planning the guest list and menu, through the preparations and by all means you should enjoy yourself at your own event.

hints to easy entertaining

Entertaining shouldn't be difficult and you don't have to have tons of things to entertain. Here is my recipe for successful entertaining:

1. Don't worry about not having "all the right things." If I waited to have all the right things, I'd never entertain.

2. Don't worry if your house or apartment isn't perfect. Hopefully your guests aren't coming for an inspection; if they are, they're not your friends! My house is far from perfect—in fact it's, shall we say, "lived in."

3. Make your guests feel comfortable. If you're uptight, they'll be uptight. Good background music that is appropriate for the event creates a very relaxing atmosphere. Alter the type of music as the evening progresses.

4. Have plenty of food and beverages. You don't want your friends going home hungry! I almost always have leftovers.

Get an inexpensive collapsible table and keep it under your bed. An old-fashioned card table or a plastic patio round table are both very inexpensive and easy to store under the bed. Use it as a prep table, or extra counter space during preparation. I'd set mine up in the living room (no room in the kitchen) while I prepped and watched TV. As party time approached I'd set it up with an inexpensive cloth and it served as a bar or serving table.

Dishes and serving pieces don't have to be expensive and they don't need to match either. Clear glass dinner plates can be found for $1.00 apiece. Similarly, attractive platters, serving dishes and utensils can be found at bargain prices. These can all be stored in a box under the bed.

Take a look around at what you have and make the most out of it; improvise. A water pitcher suddenly becomes a vase for flowers; the TV is draped with a cloth and then poised with an attractive tray of appetizers.

My friend Alex who had a small apartment in Greenwich used to have an annual holiday cocktail party. To make more room for guests, he'd move all the living room furniture into the bedroom and take the door off the apartment. Be inventive and you'll be amazed at what you can do.

Have a great time entertaining!

I think every young woman's rite of passage in to the world of grown-ups is when she hosts her first luncheon. Typically, one's first luncheon is for a special occasion. For me, it was my sister Missy's Bridesmaid Luncheon. After that, there were a slew of bridal showers and baby showers, and yes, there was the onslaught of the obligatory Tupperware-style luncheons where you're roped into hosting something so someone else can peddle *their* wares to all *your friends*—baskets, cosmetics, clothes, toys, kitchen gadgets—you name it. You know you've sat through one.

If you come to a luncheon at my house, the chances are this is the menu that will be served. It's so unbelievably easy to make and the ladies just ooh and ahh at how pretty it all is. Everyone is just so nice and acting ladylike even though they probably don't even want to be there in the first place. They're thinking of about a hundred other things they'd rather be doing right smack dab in the middle of Saturday afternoon.

How do I really feel about luncheons, you might be wondering? Well, once they get going they're usually lots of fun and I have a great time!

---

spring luncheon

gazpacho
page 73

tomato stuffed with chicken salad
page 33

fresh rolls

poached pears with raspberry coulis
page 112

This casual winter afternoon menu was created with just hanging around in mind. It's something that comes very naturally to me; in fact Bill thinks I'm an expert at it. Envision a lazy Sunday mid-winter afternoon lying on the sofa under an afghan in front of a roaring fire watching an old classic movie or a football game. You have no responsibilities for the whole day; it's too cold to do anything outside. We have frequent Sundays like this at our house. Sometimes it's just Bill and me; sometimes it's with friends.

This kind of day invites snacking—the whole day and into the evening. I get so much pleasure out of alternating between lying on the sofa and puttering around in the kitchen on a day like this. Bill will start a big pot of his chili while I prepare the filling for crispy southwestern roll-ups. Then I'll mash up avocados and make guacamole and avocado dipping sauce. I'll open up a jar of salsa, bag of chips and it's time to plop back onto the sofa and start round one of the snacking frenzy.

A while later I'll get up to stir the chili and make a batch of the Senator's bourbon hot dogs. It's time for round two of the snacking frenzy. In about an hour it's time to stir the chili again. I'll put some toffee bars in the oven and assemble and cook the crispy southwestern roll-ups. Round three of the snacking frenzy—it's chili with all the fixin's and the roll-ups with avocado dipping sauce.

The grand finale—toffee bars. What a day!

I had a whole pile of fun when I lived in Manhattan serving on the junior committees for different charitable organizations. I met lots of great people and went to some fun and some not so fun events. Heaven forbid we arrived at the event before eleven o'clock. We'd all congregate at someone's apartment for cocktails and appetizers beforehand, then in unison head out to the corner and try to hail about five taxicabs. The antipasto platter in this spread is substantial enough you feel as though you've had a meal. I love serving the Terra Chips, pretzel nibs and assorted olives because that's what they serve in the Ritz Carlton lounge and I love going there for cocktails. If you're not familiar with Terra Chips they look like wonderfully colored potato chips made from vegetables like beets and sweet potatoes.

Whether you're going to a charity event or elsewhere, this menu is nice for the cocktail hour.

pre-charity event
cocktails

raspberry brie
page 13

tortellini with pesto
page 8

antipasto platter
page 12

assorted crackers
p. 17

artichoke dip
p. 17

terra chips, pretzel nibs, assorted nuts

assorted olives

fresh strawberries

romantic dinner for
two

endive salad
page 22

cornish hen
page 48

wild rice
page 87

steamed green beans
page 90

meringue nests with
chocolate mousse and
raspberries
pages 108, 106

chocolate heart candies

You're in a new relationship; you've had a few dates already and things are going great. You have yet to have your first disagreement and you're experiencing the most pleasurable romantic bliss. ***This*** is the man of your dreams and you're telling your friends you think this is Mr. Right and could be "the one!"

You're ready to impress him with your entertaining and cooking and want that first time to be an extra special and memorable evening. This is the menu.

Create a romantic atmosphere with lots of candles and fresh flowers. Use a pretty tablecloth sprinkled with rose petals and your best china. Serve a great bottle of wine with dinner and chilled champagne with dessert. The final touch to the mood is the music. There are great CD's available at Pottery Barn that set just the right mood. Dinner at 8 features Ella Fitzgerald singing *I'm In The Mood For Love*, Nat King Cole singing *L.O.V.E*, and Joe Derise singing *A Fine Romance*. Cocktail Lounge features Mel Torme singing *You And The Night And The Music* and Keely Smith singing *What Is This Thing Called Love?* This is a sure way to win his heart forever!

Bill and I had an impromptu Valentine's Dinner Party one year. Valentine's Day was on a Saturday and we didn't want to deal with the restaurant scene so decided to have a nice quiet, casual dinner at home. Sitting around Friday night we decided to call Missy and Bob, Stacy and Carter, Ted and JoAnn and Mark (our then single friend who was wondering how he would entertain the woman he'd been dating for only a few weeks) to invite them to a last minute Valentine's Dinner Party. It turns out none of them had plans, so we ended up with an impromptu dinner party.

Everyone came casually dressed. I used this menu. I didn't have any sauce so just before serving dinner I remembered I had a couple of packets of McCormick's Hollandaise Sauce mix. I used both and added a little tarragon to half to make béarnaise sauce. I served hollandaise with the vegetables and the béarnaise with the tenderloin. Everyone thought the sauces were homemade; I fooled them but let them in on the McCormick's secret. Although the meal was very easy to make, it was still very elegant — much more elegant than our attire. We sat around the table for hours after dinner until Ted spilled half a bottle of red wine on the white linen tablecloth. We decided it was time to adjourn to the family room and sat around the fireplace while we enjoyed after-dinner drinks and a roaring fire. Sometimes impromptu parties are the best. This happened to be one of them.

dinner party for ten

roasted garlic
page 19

warm goat cheese salad
p. 23

whole roasted beef tenderloin
page 54

spiced creamy potatoes
page 85

vegetables hollandaise
page 90

chocolate roll
page 109

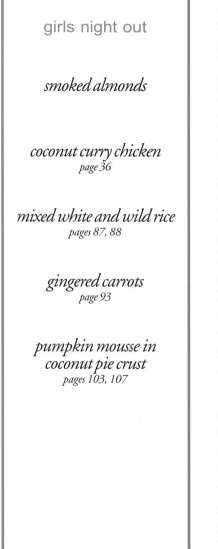

A few years ago I went to my high school reunion for St. Mary's Academy and had a blast. I ran into friends I hadn't seen in years, who all live in the area. We all vowed we wouldn't wait another ten years before getting together. Everyone gets so wrapped up being moms, wives and working professionals. How many times have you said, "Oh, we have to get together soon" and the weeks, months and years slip by and you haven't gotten together? I've been guilty many times, so a few weeks ago I had some of the girls over for dinner on a Tuesday night. It turned out it was a "sisters" night and we had all attended St. Mary's at some point in our high school careers: Kathy Ann (SMA '79) and Amy Klesius (SMA '80) and Karen (SMA '79), Kathy (SMA '80) and Michelle Day (SMA '81) and my sister Missy (SMA '75) and me (SMA '79). Did we ever laugh! It was a breeze to throw this together; I didn't go to the store until a few hours before the girls arrived and still managed to prepare everything without rushing.

Bill was out for the evening and by the time he got back home thought everyone would be long gone and I'd be doing the dishes. As it turns out it was almost midnight and several bottles of wine later when the girls realized they had to leave their fantasy world (that fantasy of having time just for themselves) and return home because they all had carpool in the morning. Thanks for a fun evening, girls and let's do it again soon!

You might think I'm crazy for suggesting a cocktail buffet for fifty when you're operating out of a shoebox of a kitchen. Trust me, it's not as difficult as it seems. One year my roommate Ellie and I had a party and had no idea how many we had invited or were showing up. We thought it would come out to about fifty. We must have had over a hundred people in and out of "Apartment 2C." At one point my friend Tom wanted to know what line he was on, referring to the subway. It was that crowded—standing room only.

If you happen to have a limited entertaining space as well as a tiny kitchen, here's the first clue: stagger the invitation times. I learned this from my friends Richard and Lisa who have an annual holiday party. They used to live in what I think must have been one of the smallest houses in Georgetown (their kitchen rivaled my kitchen in Old Town!). They would have well over fifty at their party.

They'd send out different invitations staggering the arrival times: 6:00 pm, 6:30 pm and 7:00 pm. How ingenious! The 6:00 group would be on their way out shortly after the 7:00 group began to arrive. This kept the crowd manageable. In addition to staggered arrival times, they'd put up a tarp that covered their tiny backyard and rented a space heater. If you're creative, you can make it work!

Pick up cooked and peeled shrimp from your local market. Serve chilled in a bowl with cocktail sauce.

cocktail buffet for fifty

brie with prosciutto
page 14

sliced beef tenderloin
page 54

mayonnaise and horseradish

sliced roasted turkey breast
page 50

tortellini and pesto dip
page 8

shrimp bowl with cocktail sauce

grandma dexter's pound cake
page 99

decadent chocolate cake
page 100

grandma dexter's butter cookies
page 98

fresh fruit tray

Every year my parents host a Thanksgiving Evening stop-by for friends and family. And it is literally just that—come as you are anytime after 7:30 pm; no Rsvp necessary. Friends and family come over to launch the holiday season and have a turkey sandwich, a piece of their favorite dessert and the first Christmas carols of the season.

We still have the traditional Thanksgiving fare. Relatives congregate at someone else's house for the big feast in the early afternoon. Then we head over to my parents'. When Grandma Dexter was still alive she would do all the baking for an entire week before—her apple pie, pound cake, mince pie, butter cookies, pecan pie, chocolate pecan pie and little pecan tarts—were the staples at the dessert table.

Don't let a tiny kitchen, deter you from having a crowd for Thanksgiving. This is a great alternative and a way to overcome the dilemmas involved with having a large crowd: where will I seat everyone? what will I do about enough china and silverware? how will I keep all the food warm? my refrigerator isn't big enough! I don't have enough burners to cook all the side dishes!

This is a cold buffet (a little bit of a scaled down version of what my mother makes, to accommodate a tiny kitchen) and many of the items can be made earlier in the week. The decadent chocolate cake and Grandma Dexter's pound cake can be made the week before and frozen until the day of. The cranberry-orange relish and hard sauce can be made three days before. The mince pie and apple pie can be made the day before as can the overnight meringues. Get snow-flake rolls or parker house rolls from your local bakery the day before. Make the pumpkin chiffon pie and let two turkey breasts roast in the morning while you're watching the Macy's Day Parade. You'll have everything out of the oven by noon and can head out and enjoy your day.

My mother puts this spread on each year and everyone who comes has his or her favorites. My Uncle John's favorite is apple pie and Aunt Loretta's is the pumpkin chiffon pie. Matthew, Katie, Mary Rose and my cousin Dawn come for the decadent chocolate cake. Mine is a turkey sandwich smothered in mayonnaise with lots of salt and a piece of pumpkin chiffon pie. Ernie comes for the mince pie, Bill comes for the pecan pie and some come just for the bourbon and scotch. My friend Jimmy—he comes for everything. One year my mother skimped a little on the desserts—I think she left out the pecan pie and mince pie and some cookies. Boy, were some folks disappointed.

This is a great tradition and wonderful way to start the holiday season with friends and family.

index

Special thanks to everyone at Fannon Color Printing in Alexandria, Virginia.